EVALU...

AND

ASSESSING

FOR

LEARNING

REVISED EDITION

DUNCAN HARRIS AND CHRIS BELL

 **NP**

Kogan Page Ltd, London
Nichols Publishing Company,
New Jersey

Dedicated to all the learners and colleagues with whom we have been, are, and hope to be associated.

First published in 1986
Second edition published in 1990
First published in paperback 1994
Reprinted in 2002

Kogan Page Limited
120 Pentonville Road
London N1 9JN

© Duncan Harris and Chris Bell 1986, 1990, 1994

Typeset by Saxon Graphics Ltd, Derby
Printed and bound in Great Britain by Biddles Ltd, Guildford and King's Lynn

British Library Cataloguing in Publication Data

A CIP record for this book is available from the British Library

ISBN 0 7494 1301 8

Contents

Acknowledgements

We would like to offer our thanks and appreciation to all those who have contributed in one way or another to the development of this book. To mention them all by name would be too daunting a task, but in particular we wish to thank:

- The learners and colleagues who, over a long period of time, have helped us form and develop our ideas.

- All those who have commented on the first edition.

- Our patient and (again) long suffering publishers.

- Jan, Gail and Mary who spent many hours transforming the vagaries of our writing into readable text.

Duncan Harris
Chris Bell

Preface

Since the first edition was published five years ago, much has happened in the world of assessment and evaluation. Assessment for certification has moved much more towards a criterion-referenced or competency-based approach, although higher education has yet to move as much in this direction as other phases of education and training. Evaluation is often viewed as being synonymous with accountability, audits and quality assurance. We feel that the current volume is even more important to help put these approaches into the context of helping learners to learn and even raising some questions about current trends.

Education and training continue to move away from the use of the human mind as a store for information towards using the mind for sorting, synthesizing, discriminating and applying information which is already stored elsewhere. There is also continued movement away from assessing which is based on examinations taken on a particular day to classify, order and rank people, towards assessing which looks for competency and personal achievements over a period of time. The onus for learning is being shifted from the teacher to the learner. The roles of teacher and learner are rapidly changing, with the teacher being seen as a manager and organizer of learning rather than a presenter of knowledge.

The book is divided into five sections. Each section can be read independently. The order in which we have presented the sections is our preferred order, but we are conscious that readers may prefer alternative orders. Many cross-references to other sections are given.

Throughout the book, we have used the word 'learner' to indicate anyone who is in a learning situation; it could be a trainer finding out about new training methods, a teacher finding out about new assessment methods or the more obvious trainees, students and pupils. By 'teacher' we mean anyone organizing a learning experience for others; it could be a student organizing a syndicate with other students, a trainee presenting a case study or, once again, the more obvious lecturers, trainers, tutors and teachers.

In order to make the reading of the book easier we have departed from the normal academic practice of giving references in the text. We have provided an annotated bibliography of further reading at the end of each section. References in these lists are intended for the reader who wants to take further a particular topic or idea we have introduced. In some case, references present an alternative or complementary perspective to that which we have adopted. We have tried to acknowledge the sources of many of our ideas by including a bibliography at the end of the book. We apologize if we have inadvertently omitted other references. Any omission is entirely our responsibility.

At the beginning of each section we have provided a conventional listing of content together with a 'mind map' display of the section and major interlinks. Throughout the book we have included brief case studies known to us. Where we are aware of the case study having been reported in the literature, the source is included in the bibliography either at the end of the section or in the general bibliography at the end of the book.

Because we consider that more will be learned and experienced through being actively involved in learning, and we perceive the main readership as being professionals who are not working alone, we have included suggestions for group work at the end of each section. We have also included 'difficulties and criticisms' at the end of each section which highlight problems associated with the proposals that we have made.

We anticipate the readers of the book to include:

- mature students on advanced courses;

- tutors of advanced courses;

- groups of teachers undertaking curriculum development on a local or regional/county basis; and

- groups of trainers undertaking development of training materials.

In this edition we have expanded the case studies, and rewritten and extended the sections on types of learners, styles of evaluating, self-assessment, peer assessment, learners' roles, teachers' roles, management and dissemination and values. We have added a new section on matching the system to the environment and also made many minor changes to the text. The cross-referencing in the text has been extended and many recent references added while retaining most of the previous ones.

We wish to note that the book expounds the current views of the authors. Many colleagues, students and writers have contributed to these views, and we gratefully acknowledge their ideas. We realize that many alternative perspectives exist and do not intend what we have written to be taken as definitive; rather we hope to encourage people to think, discuss and try alternatives.

Section 1. Needs of the learner

Section 1. Needs of the learner

Section 1. Needs of the learner

Introduction

Learning can be related to four theories of teaching:

- Transfer theory where knowledge is treated as a commodity to be transferred from one person to another.

- Shaping theory where the learner is shaped or moulded to a pre-determined pattern

- Travelling theory where the subject is seen as a terrain to be explored; the more difficult hills and mountains help to give a better viewpoint and the teacher is like a travelling companion or guide.

- Growing theory where the intellectual and emotional development of the learner are the focus.

In this book we shall concentrate on the growing theory, but aspects of the other three will be apparent. Learners have not only their own development to cope with but also have to take account of interaction with other people and the ethos of the local and national societies in which they live. There is a tendency towards competence based approaches, particularly in the USA and UK.

Types of learners

Some learners prefer to have information presented to them one step at a time in a linear or serial form. Other learners find learning easier when they can see the 'whole picture' to begin with so that they can rearrange the various parts into a pattern which makes sense to them. The former type of learners are often called 'serialist' and the latter type 'holist'.

Serialist learners generally favour linear types of notes whilst holists may favour patterned (or coral) type notes. For this reason, we have provided both styles of summary at the start of each section. However, the patterned notes we have drawn present our own interpretation of the section content. Other people may form a different picture of the content and consequently would produce a different patterned note.

Many learners are able to switch from one style to another, often according to the structure of the learning under consideration. Perhaps this ability to switch could be described as a 'patchwork' style. Some learners are only able to operate in one or other of the styles. Do we help them feel more secure with the other style, or do we adopt material and how it is used to the preferred styles of individual learners?

There are many other ways of 'classifying' learning style. One which is particularly useful follows from the work of Honey and Mumford (1982). Here, a four-fold classification is used:

- activist

- pragmatist

- reflector

- theorist.

Although some learners will not show bias towards any one style, others may show a strong tendency towards one or more of the styles. Preferred styles can be assessed by using the 'Learning Styles Questionnaire'. Plotting results on a grid similar to that shown in Figure 1.1 gives a graphic representation of a learner's preferences.

There are important implications for teaching (ie providing a learning situation). Learners exhibiting different preferred styles are likely to learn more effectively from different situations. For example:

Activists learn best when:

- there are new experiences, problems and opportunities

- they become engrossed in the 'here and now'

- there is excitement

- things change rapidly

- they lead the learning activities

- they are given freedom in their learning

- they are set challenges.

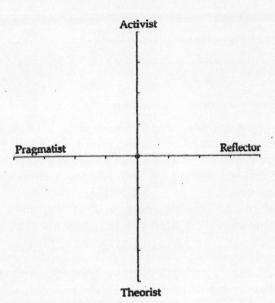

Figure 1.1 *Learner-preference grid*

Reflectors learn best when:

- they are encouraged to observe and think about activities
- they can take a 'back seat' role
- they are given time to reflect and consider
- they work in a detailed and painstaking way
- learning experiences are well structured.

Theorists learn best when:

- they can organise learning within a personal system or model
- there is time for methodical exploration of ideas and situations
- they have a chance to question and probe
- they are intellectually stretched
- learning is structured with clear aims
- learning appears logical and rational
- they think first, analyse and then generalise
- they are required to understand.

Pragmatists learn best when:

- there appears to be immediate relevance to the learning
- learning is practically biased
- they can practise and apply learning
- they can copy or emulate a model or theory.

Learners may be unaware of their own preferred style and may need help in identifying that which is most comfortable for them. In addition to the 'Learning Styles Questionnaire', some of the activities at the end of this section are designed to help identify the preferred learning styles of learners.

In order to encourage learners to try new styles, it is helpful if teachers can use varied strategies of notes and presentations, and persuade learners to try new methods, share their ideas with other learners and evaluate the strengths and weaknesses themselves. Some institutions adopt a policy of all teachers spending time on learning skills and study methods in relation to their own subjects. Other institutions give help during pastoral, tutorial or counselling activities. One of the authors institutions provides a series of free leaflets on study skills to all its learners. The purpose is to help learners to gain confidence in their ability to learn, and therefore to learn more effectively.

We return to the ideas noted above in several parts of the book. In particular, learning how to learn is discussed on page 000.

Learning activities

Let us consider four members of the same family, Pat, Norma(n), Nick(y) and Jo(e). Jo(e) drives a fire engine, Norma(n) is a journalist, Pat is a coal miner operating equipment at the coal face and Nick(y) is a social worker. Each of them uses certain knowledge and routines which they have memorised. Each of them has information and data which they have to decode and use. Each of them has to create solutions to problems. Each of them has to work within a team. So each has the need to meet certain attainments and competencies. We suggest that during learning, learners need to carry out a number of activities, including:

- memorising

● decoding

● creating

● loving.

In a learning context, activity may be in the form of remembering by heart (memorising), reading, selecting and organizing information to write an assignment (decoding), heuristic and creative activities (creating) and working within a group, developing and facilitating group interactions (loving). Let us consider each of these learning activities in the context of a simplified learning experience.

A new stereo cassette deck, amplifier and speakers have been bought by a family. On unpacking the boxes, they find that there are no instructions for operating the cassette deck. On the front panel of the deck are a variety of push button switches, each with a symbol. After connecting the equipment, the family discuss the meaning of the symbols. Each has their own ideas. Norma (whose present the deck is) not only attempts to decode the meaning of each symbol, but also has to decode the often conflicting ideas coming from the rest of the family.

Norma makes a series of decisions, and tries to operate the deck. Some decisions were correct (had the desired outcome) and others were wrong. Further decoding occurs in the light of her experiences. The meaning of symbols becomes clearer and can now be memorised by the whole family.

Jack has just learnt to read. To help him operate the deck, Norma creates a set of simple written labels which she sticks above the controls. Norma has decoded information from a variety of sources, memorised the use of the deck and has used this information to create an alternative set of instructions.

The stereo equipment now works. However, Jack wants his bedtime story tapes played, Norma wants to listen to some folk music whereas both parents want to listen to classical music. The family need to readjust to a new potential source of conflict: a loving activity!

We consider each of the learning activities in greater depth. They will be referred to at various parts of the book.

Memorising

Drivers of taxi-cabs, buses and coaches in large cities are often required to pass a test of knowledge of streets, one way systems etc. Such a test may be required annually. Pilots of passenger aircraft are required to remember routines both for regular activities and for emergencies. Musicians, typists and sportsmen are required to remember sequences and positions of body, hands and fingers to enhance speed and accuracy. Linguists need to learn vocabulary, master grammar and syntax. Actors need to remember cues and lines. Lawyers need to remember case histories.

Many facets of our lives require immediate recall of facts, sequences of ideas or physical actions. Although memorising and rote learning are becoming less popular in current educational thinking, there are still many requirements for memorising; it is in the context of meaningful rote learning and memorising that this section is elaborated.

The learner needs routines, changes to maintain interest, techniques for learning (which have to be adapted to each individual), assignments and assessment. The teacher needs to add to these interactions, systematic evaluating of problems, successes, and new ideas in order to modify present strategies and identify future ones. It is clear that assignments, assessing and evaluating are a crucial part of the negotiated process of learning between teacher and learner. They are a part of the means of providing immediate short term motivation for the learner, and feedback for learners and teachers.

In memorising or rote learning of knowledge, a variety of strategies can be adopted, for example:

- mnemonics (eg. ROYGBIV colours of the visible spectrum: red, orange, yellow, green, blue, indigo, violet)
- picture storage (eg. where a familiar room/scene is remembered and facts are located in particular drawers, or on a particular tree)
- using numbers (eg. where the person remembers numbers better than words and associates ideas with number sequences in order to recall them).

These mechanisms are used in order to overcome the limitations of the human memory. In over-simplified terms the human mind can recall about seven different items for discrimination at any one time. In order to extend the memory we group, classify and cluster: remembering seven classes of things, the first is subdivided into say four, and so on. The classification needs to be relevant to the learner, and to that being learned (for example many actors find lines easier to remember when they are associated with actions, intonations).

The types of assessment most applicable for memorising include:

- true/false questions

- multiple choice questions
- repetition (eg. being required to write in extended form that which is provided)
- completion questions
- essay questions where the assumption is recall.

We consider these in more detail in section 3. For movement (psychomotor) learning, assessment may involve accurate repetition at increasing speeds or levels of control.

What seems to be important in meaningful rote learning is that the learning makes sense in relation to the experiences of the learner. The examples that we have given relate to people's means of employment or to enabling them to be allowed to do something (eg. drive a car). In providing a learning situation, a crucial aspect is that the organizer must know the existing cognitive or psychomotor structures for the individual learner (or at very worst for the group) and to use and build upon this. Without assessing and evaluating, cooperating and nego-tiating with learners the jug is used to fill the glass with meaningless repetition.

Decoding

Decoding is a popular form of learning at some levels, particularly with younger children, in higher education and with learners learning on their own (what we have called mediated self-learning in section 5). Imagine a typical learning situation in some institutions. At the end of a lecture, a set of problems are given out which are designed to build upon information presented during the lecture. A number of books and a video recording are mentioned as being useful to study before answering the problems. The suggested books, lecture material and video recording all present information about the subject of the problems, but:

- several of the books are very complicated, each presenting different parts of the 'whole' picture
- two of the books appear to be in conflict over certain points
- the video recording only presents a small area of information; it was designed to be used as part of a distance study course.

Learners presented with the scenario described above are faced with a number of possibilities; for example they could:

- ask the lecturer for clarification (the 'right answer')
- decode the various sources of information, perhaps using one source to help explain another
- give up, perhaps finding it too difficult or unmotivating to decode with a view to learning new information.

In the above example, decoding involves synthesizing information from different sources, perhaps discussing with fellow learners whilst so doing. Decoding is equally needed by many when presented with symbols (eg. map, tape deck), or complex or jargon ridden information. For example:

In highly structured linear and cumulative subjects the decision algorithm is easier to control than those subjects where value judgements are involved.
or
Plug type cup testers suitable for pressure testing the BOP equipment is installed on all casing strings.
or
In some countries, people nod their heads meaning 'no' whilst shaking the head means 'yes'. A person from a country which uses nodding for yes will have to adapt. The decoding will take time.

All the above examples may require a considerable amount of decoding, depending upon the pre-knowledge of the reader: what is perfectly clear to the writer could be meaningless to the reader.

The process of finding information, ideas, evidence and collating and organizing these aspects is a complex task, often overlooked by the 'expert' teacher who has already been initiated. The style of assessing which is applicable for these needs of learners is different from those outlined in the previous part, although they obviously overlap, relate together and share common techniques. Here, the focus of questions, essays or assignments will be on assessing the learner's ability to take and restructure information. 'Comprehension' type assessment is a good example, where learners read (or watch) something and then have to interpret its meaning when answering questions. Case study and role play are also possibilities, particularly when body signals are important (for example in much foreign language teaching).

The driving test in the U.K. consists of several elements. The learner driver has to know off by heart the meaning of all the traffic signs and road markings in the Highway Code. In the test a selection of these are asked using miniature symbols. By memorising the symbols and their meaning the learner should be able to pass this part of the test. The learner also has to be able to start and stop the car smoothly, do an emergency stop, reverse into a restricted width opening or road, and turn the car round in a road (the 3 point turn). All of these manoeuvres are memorised psychomotor sequences where practice enables satisfactory performance. Most of the remainder of the test is driving in normal traffic where decoding will be necessary because the conditions are unpredictable. Seldom will the learner driver be required to act creatively unless they and the tester are strangers in the area (a case is known to one of the authors!)

Creating

Project work and creative work have been particularly used with younger age groups and in higher education. They have been less common in the high school/secondary school except in certain creative subjects such as art and in the industrial arts and technology.

In real life there are many occupations which obviously require this sort of expertise; there are also many where initiative is required but the educational system has prevented its development. The obvious examples are: artist, architect, detective. Also some less obvious ones: messenger, secretary and taxi-cab driver.

Initiative, creative opportunities, the need to search for resources relating to a topic of your own choice are associated much more with education up to the age of 11. After this age there is a tendency to move towards a subject based education where the teacher becomes a subject expert rather than a pedagogic expert. The learner finds a different expectation where the requirement is to remember, to comprehend pre-conceived concepts or to accept existing critical review. Obviously this is an exaggerated picture of education and training after the age of eleven, but it is still the dominant view.

In learning situations which are aiming at creative, project type work where initiative and willingness to try out ideas are essential, the role of assessment is rather different from those already outlined. Generally the learner has a need for a high level of support and confidence boosting in the early stages; but the support needs to be gradually withdrawn. It sounds easy, but unfortunately learners have very different time scales for this withdrawal of support. Some may require the support to be withdrawn fairly early in the process and a more critical view taken by the teacher. For others it may be difficult to persuade them to 'paddle their own canoe' at any time.

The assessment becomes very much an integral part of the learning. There are a set of key questions that need asking early in the process:

- What are the purposes of the learning experience?

- What does the learner think are the purposes of particular work that has been agreed or allocated?

- What are the purposes of the assessment procedure that has been agreed or negotiated?

- What is the relationship between the learning experience and the assessment. (Has the assessment become the whole organization of the experience?)

The type of work outlined here is probably one of the most difficult to assess without losing sight of the purpose of learning. It would appear that very often negotiated contracts and agreements are one way of overcoming some of these difficulties and of providing motivation to the learner. However there must be very careful consideration given whether the assessment should be entirely associated with the end product or with the process, or even with both aspects. The assessment itself can also be viewed in a number of possible ways:

- impression

- objective

- contract

- ranking.

These are discussed further in section 3.

Loving

Much work in real life is carried out in groups of people. Not only do the group have to do a particular series of tasks but also need to adjust to other members of the group. The educational system has not incorporated this as an important aspect except in certain specialist training in higher education and training (eg. Psychology, Management) where it is carried out at a fairly sophisticated level. However we argue that it is an important and inherent need in any educational system and also in many aspects of training. Learners need to find out quite explicitly how to work in groups. The associated assessing and evaluating needs to take account of these requirements.

Work within groups can be considered to have the following purposes:

- to promote understanding of a body of knowledge
- to elucidate misunderstanding and difficulty
- to practice skills: intellectual, verbal, computational and interpersonal
- to practise application of principles in familiar and unfamiliar situations
- to explore personal and professional attitudes and values
- to enable a two way exchange of information.

It can be seen that these purposes cover everything from a pair of learners working out a mathematics problem together, to a group of people learning how best to work together as a team. One of the interesting things about working in groups (up to a size of about 16 in number) is the way that assessment and evaluation become a much more natural and integrated part of the whole learning process rather than something that is added on as an extra and imposed from outside by a teacher or an external examining body.

In a very simplified form the group has two main functions:

- the completion of a task within the limitations of the members of the group (a 'task centred' function)
- the mutual support within the group in order to carry out whatever task is in hand to the mutual satisfaction of the group (a 'process centred' function).

It is crucial that a group learns that these are competing requirements and it is therefore necessary for the group to stay together as long as possible in order to get a feel of the learning requirements and of each other. We have made some suggestions about how groups can be encouraged to function in section 2 (see page 51). It is recommended that some or all of these techniques are used with students whatever the learning or training area in which they are involved.

Considering the two types of group focus (task centred and process centred) let us consider in more detail the implications for, and needs of, the learners. The task centred group will focus on aspects such as:

- the application of principles
- acquiring and practising skills (this could include the skills of working in a group)
- promoting understanding (for example why work as an individual when the discussion and argument with other learners may help to overcome learning

difficulties? But the learners need to change their attitude that learning and life are all about being competitive and secretive, there are social as well as educational implications.)

The process centred group will focus more on the following aspects:

● the understanding of inter-personal interaction

● the development of group skills

● the development of professional skills in communication

● the understanding of personal bias

● exploratory or creative problem solving.

The characteristics shown by members of a group in the task area will be communication, evaluation and control. It should be immediately clear that the two focuses overlap. The recognition of members' perspectives and roles in the task area can be seen by activities such as giving suggestions, giving opinions, asking for opinions, asking for suggestions and giving or asking for orientation.

The characteristics of the process centred approach are decision making, tension reduction and group integration. Recognition would be by looking for antagonism, solidarity, tension and tension release, agreeing and disagreeing. It should be clear that different learners will have different needs according to their previous experiences. It becomes necessary as far as possible for the individual and other members of the group to identify each learner's needs rather than using a continuous series of interventions from the teacher. However the skills and methods of working in a group cannot be assumed, they must be nurtured. However because the learner's view of learning is coloured by previous experience there will be a clear need to enable the group to function more efficiently in this mode.

A group of teachers attending an in service course on evaluating were asked to write down briefly how they used assessment in their own school. In pairs each member introduced themselves with a very brief outline of the school. Pairs then looked for differences in what each had previously written. In fours, groups tried to identify any consensus. In the process so far the learners (in this case teachers) were finding out and learning from one another.

The course leaders now asked each group of four to report one use for assessment. Uses were recorded on the overhead projector, and the process was continued until all were identified. Now not only were the learners hearing about other people's views but also the course leaders (ie. the teachers) have found out where the course members are in their thinking so that the course can be built on those bases rather than either repeating ground that is already familiar or jumping too far ahead. The process has enabled the course leaders to identify the pre-requisites whilst also encouraging the learners to learn from one another in their first meeting.

(Further details of this technique (snowballing) are given in section 2.)

Suggested group activities

1. What is good learning and bad learning?

The question is used as a basis for the group to exchange and share ideas. In order to help the group, raise the two ideas separately. For example, 'think of a good learning experience that you have had', 'think of a bad learning experience you have had'. In order to help them to focus their ideas it is worth saying that these experiences can be in any context (eg. hobbies, school). Use snowballing, nominal group technique or buzz groups to help the group discussion (see section 2 for further details of these techniques).

2. How do you take notes?

Ask learners to bring notes with them and go into pairs immediately to explain to one another why they took their notes that way and how they will use them. After about 10 minutes ask the group to move into fours (as in snowballing). Ask them to identify good and bad practice in taking notes.

3. How do you use your time?

A series of questions can be given to each learner. The learners are asked to mark those that apply to them. When individuals have completed their list they move into pairs and compare with another learner looking for differences. On completion of this, fours are asked to identify whether each question matters and to come to some sort of consensus on the use of time. Fours report in the normal way for snowballing (see page 52). This approach is described in detail in Gibbs (1981).

4. How do you develop your own information system?

Ask learners to bring their own system (eg. a card or computer index of references they have found valuable) and explain it to another learner. After this they move into fours looking for good and bad characteristics of information systems. Reporting is carried out in the normal way.

5. How important is social interaction?

A paper may be given to the learners for them to read before they meet. At the meeting, learners are not permitted to criticise the paper. The first stage is to identify any parts of the paper that cannot be understood or which are considered to need clarification. The learners then explain to one another their difficulties. The procedure goes on to identify the main issues in the paper, to discuss these individually, the way in which the paper fits into the group member's own experience, and the application of the paper in the present context. Only then can the paper be criticised, and the group look at its own performance. This method is called 'Learning Through Discussion'; see Hill (1978) for further details.

6. How do learners differ?

A free discussion on section 1 of this book could be used.

7. Learner at home, tutor at home, learner wants help. How can the help be arranged?

Either use role play where pairs argue out the basis between themselves and then report their suggestions to the rest of the group, or use brainstorming (see page 54).

Difficulties and criticisms

There are basic educational conflicts in the ideas that have been outlined in this chapter. The behavioural and contractual type of learning tends to assume an end point specification where the product is assessed. So for example if a learner is given a project to do with a period of time in which to complete it, then the end point approach will only assess the report or the artefact that comes at the end of the process. However in the process type of approach the assessment would focus primarily on the way in which the problem was approached, the strategies used, the decisions made, the basis of those decisions, the evaluation of alternate strategies etc.

Is education about developing the individual or ensuring that the individual fits into society? The former will focus on the attributes, strengths and weaknesses of the individual without attempting to mould that individual, whereas the latter will want to mould the individual into conformity. Perhaps the classic dilemma is in teacher training: is the teacher to be trained to fit into the existing system (the 'sitting by Nellie' approach), developed as an individual to work to the best of their ability within their own personality, or even to be a radical change agent for society? Obviously these have very different assessment assumptions. The example can be transferred into any aspect of learning where the learner is expected to follow and learn what is prescribed (at worst, rote learning existing ideas and concepts); the second would be where an attempt is made to enable the learner to adapt their learning style to fit their own needs and there would not be an expectation of rote learning, the third may be the learner required to question the whole basis of the subject or learning.

We have suggested a style of learning based on negotiation. This style is fine with willing learners, but what about unwilling and unmotivated learners? Unfortunately the change in approach is often introduced to learners who are already alienated from learning. Both categories of learners will need a lot of help initially in order to take on responsibility for their own learning because the general trend is still towards providing prepackaged learning whether on the chalkboard, in hand-outs, in books or in multi-media packages.

A teacher has to be a problem solver with a group of human beings yet much teacher training is still carried out in a didactic mode to serried rows of learners in lecture theatres, with little attention paid to heuristic methods of learning. At the end of their teacher training course they will have to take on the responsibility for their own problem solving for which they have had little in the way of training or education.

Negotiated learning also depends on who is the major partner in the negotiation: who decides on the content, level, means of learning, time to be spent, assessment etc.? Certification is also a problem; can negotiated learning be acceptable in external certification? Certainly while the focus on certification is on competitive assessment there is some difficulty in negotiating except in the best way to beat the assessors! However with a movement towards criterion-referenced measurement and towards profiles of achievement there is more potential for negotiated learning.

The development of the learner as identified above, involves decisions about the learner's strengths and weaknesses. Who controls the building on the strengths and building up from the weaknesses? Assessment has a key role to play in this process. However caution should be exercised, there is not sufficient evidence to support the idea that teacher developed assessment procedures can pin-point actual learner weaknesses by themselves. In a subject like mathematics, there may be several different ways (or algorithms) of devising the answer to a particular question. Where simple questions (eg. multiple choice) are used, only one of these algorithms may have been taken into account in the grading scheme; the learner who uses a different algorithm may well have incorrect diagnosis of errors.

In a negotiated learning situation, assessment is not remote from the learner but something about which the learner and the teacher talk, the learner identifying the sort of strategy that they have taken. If it appears that the time involved in such negotiation is beyond the staff-learner ratio, then the learners themselves can take some of the responsibility for part of their own assessment. In this case it is important that the teacher does see learner's work on a systematic and regular basis.

Another key area of difficulty is the influence of the subject or discipline. The learner is involved in the process of learning; that process depends on their own stage of development and also their previous experience. Unfortunately much subject-based learning does not take into account the development of the learner. The subject is constructed around content, concepts, and frameworks. It is taught in a fixed time scale often ignoring the development of the learner, at worst in a lock-step-time oriented basis. The learning may be more suitable for a fixed learning variable time basis, but this requires a totally different idea of the organization of teaching and assessment. It is often assumed that only mastery-type learning is suitable for a variable time approach. There are many distance study courses around the world in a complete range of disciplines. Few of these operate on a fixed time basis in the way that institutionalized education and training do. Why should the people on distance study courses have that type of learning almost exclusively for themselves? What is the potential in institutionalised education and training?

Annotated bibliography

Anania, J (1983)
The Influence of Instructional Conditions on Student Learning and Achievement
Evaluation in Education, 7, 1, 1-92.
This long paper identifies a study carried out in an American school. The focus of the study was the human potential for learning. The study identified that most learners had very big capabilities for learning. Three styles of learning environment were considered – conventional teaching, mastery learning and a tutoring approach. The latter two approaches which are elaborated involved high participation by learners, cues to and evidence of success. 'Almost every' student had a very high capacity for learning once they identified a belief in their own ability. The two approaches depended heavily on assessment for learning.

Ausubel, D P, Novak, J D and Hanesian, H (1978)
Educational Psychology: a Cognitive View
New York: Holt, Rinehart and Winston.
A detailed discussion of the ways in which individuals learn. The book provides much information of direct relevance to improving the quality of learning, from structuring learning materials and aids to analysing learning styles.

Bawden, R and Valentine, J (1984)
Learning to be a Capable Systems Agriculturalist
Programmed Learning and Educational Technology, 21, 4, 273-287.
The course described focusses not only on Systems Agriculturalists but also on those agriculturalists being autonomous learners and effective communicators aimed at helping others and building up good interpersonal relationships. The course uses two learning strategies in two contexts. The contexts are staff initiative (gradually decreasing) and

student initiative (gradually increasing); the latter involves the use of cooperative groups. The assessment is based around a student and employer initiated competency profile including peer and self evaluation of learning.

Bigge, M L (1982)
Learning Theories for Teachers
New York: Harper and Row.
A comprehensive and balanced treatment of early and contemporary learning theories and their implications for teachers and trainers. The roles of teachers and learners are discussed in the context of theoretical models.

Bloom, B S et al (1956)
Taxonomy of Educational Objectives Handbook 1: Cognitive Domain
New York: McKay.
A proposal for a taxonomy based on the analysis of a large number of assessments at various levels of education in the USA. The framework of the basic 6 levels is Knowledge, Comprehension, Application, Analysis, Synthesis and Evaluation. Examples of objectives and assessments are given in the book.

Boud, D, Keogh, R and Walker, D (eds) (1985)
Developing Student Autonomy in Learning
London: Kogan Page.
In the last decade, experience-based learning has been increasingly used in a variety of teaching and learning contexts. This book brings together theoretical insights into reflexion which have occurred across various fields and links them with practical examples of implementation in particular educational situations.

Brindley, B (1989)
Complete Guide to Competency Based Education
Englewood Cliffs N J, Prentice Hall
The book outlines the expectation, structure, design and assessment related to competency based approaches.

Buzan, T (1982)
Use Your Head
London: British Broadcasting Corporation.

The book explains the latest discoveries about the human brain and helps the reader to understand more clearly how their mind works. It includes tests and exercises to improve reading power, memory, studying effectively, solving problems more readily and ways of thinking. The well knowm mind maps (otherwise known as coral diagrams, patterned notes, etc.) are a feature of the book.

Entwistle, N (1981)
Styles of Teaching and Learning : an Integrated Outline of Educational Psychology
London: Wiley.
Provides an overview of those aspects of educational psychology related to an understanding of how learners learn. The book is a good starting place for someone new to this area of psychology or who wants a summary of research findings. Many references are provided.

Fox, D (1983)
Personal theories of education *Studies in Higher Education* 8, 2, 151–63
This paper provides the four theories of teaching: transfer theory, shaping theory, travelling theory and growing theory.

Gagne, R M (1985)
The Conditions of Learning
New York: Holt, Rinehart and Winston.
Expounds the use of a particular learning hierarchy which can be used to analyse learning and the curriculum. Ideas presented provide useful starting points when considering how to structure learning aids and materials to improve learning.

Hill, W F (1978)
Learning Thru' Discussion
Palo Alto: Fearon.
A small book which gives a ten stage system for organizing discussion particularly related to discussion around papers that are provided. The system involves focusing on problems of comprehension and the main messages of the paper, leaving the criticism until near the end. The final focus is on the group's performance.

Honey, P and Mumford, A (1982)
The Manual of Learning Styles

Maidenhead: Peter Honey.
A manual aimed particularly at managers, but of interest to all learners. The authors suggest four learning styles: activists, reflectors, theorists and pragmatists. The characteristics of all are elaborated and a questionnaire is provided to enable a learner to classify their own style. The manual aims to enable learners to develop as all rounders.

Jonassen, D H (1985)
Learning Strategies : a New Educational Technology
Programmed Learning and Educational Technology, 22, 1, 26-34.
The paper addresses the more cognitive theories and assumptions and their implementation in educational technology. The failure to provide generalizable instructional techniques has forced us to shift our emphasis to what learners do. Educational technologies need to become learner-oriented. The goal of new technologies, such as learning strategies, is to promote independent, self motivated learners who are capable of initiating, selecting, and using appropriate strategies for acquiring, retaining and using knowledge.

Rumelhart, D E and Norman D A (1981)
Analogical Processes in Learning. In Anderson. J R (ed) *Cognitive Skills and their Aquisition*
Hellodale N J: Lawrence Erlbaum Associates.
Introduces the ideas of declarative and procedural learning which feature in much literature in USA.

Slavin, R E (1983)
Cooperative Learning
New York: Longman.
One of several books in USA which advocates the use of and effectiveness of cooperative (group) learning.

Whittrock, M C (1974)
Learning as a Generative Activity
Educational Psychologist 11, 87-95
The idea of generative learning is described, where learners are active in their own learning.

Section 2. Evaluating: fitting the system to the needs of learners

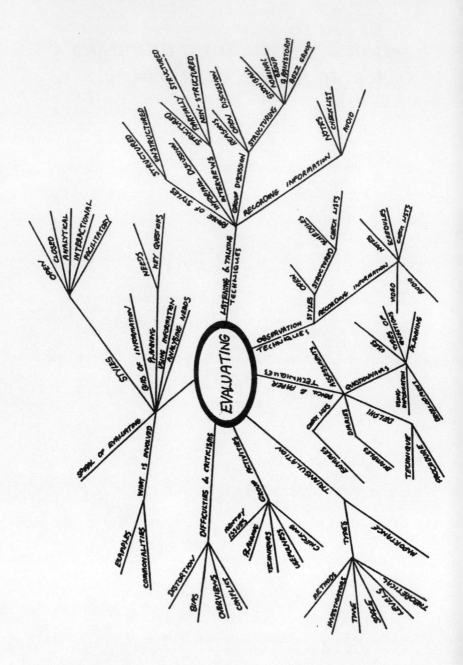

Section 2. Evaluating: fitting the system to the needs of learners

Section 2. Evaluating: fitting the system to the needs of learners

Introduction

Throughout the text we are emphasizing learning as a cooperative venture between 'learner' and 'teacher'. Nowhere is such cooperation more important than in the evaluation process which we consider should be an integral part of course design, implementation and post course reflexion. Traditionally the before, during and after phases of evaluating have been given the labels 'needs-analysis', 'formative evaluation' and 'summative evaluation'.

Needs analysis (or preparatory evaluation) is a necessary part of course design, although often discussed less in educational than training environments. Needs analysis is as important when considering an individual lesson or seminar as it is when designing a new distance learning package. Mismatch between the learner and content or approach of learning is unlikely to optimize learning and may well lead to alienation. As we move towards open and self-learning, then needs analysis becomes increasingly important for the learners to undertake themselves: what do I need to learn? what do I want to learn? how may I best learn? where may I best learn?

Evaluating during the learning process (often termed formative evaluation) is important for learners and teachers alike, aiding the teacher in fine-tuning (or hole plugging and patching) and the learner in becoming more involved in, and aware of, the learning process. In addition, the communication which should arise naturally from such evaluation is a vital aid to the learners and teachers becoming more aware both of themselves and of each others views, problems and expectations. It should be a sharing process .

Evaluating subsequent to learning (often termed summative evaluation) is necessary for providing information to both learners and teachers about learning which has occurred, perhaps comparing it with that which was intended. Factors enabling and constraining the learning process may also be identified. Such evaluating can provide the learner and teacher with information about what learning is still necessary to achieve particular goals, and the teacher about development of future courses.

In this section we discuss the processes of planning and organizing evaluating and consider various styles and techniques which can be used at the different phases of learning. Throughout, emphasis is on small scale applications where the aim is understanding and improving learning/teaching. For readers who require further details of techniques sign-posted in this section, texts noted in the bibliography at the end should form useful starting points.

Needs analysis

In most cases the learning content, sequence and environment are chosen by teachers and trainers. The decisions are often based on the opinions of those teachers or trainers, sometimes using ideas generated from government agencies (eg. National Curriculum, National Vocational Qualification in UK), researchers or the requirement of employers. Unfortunately, young learners or young trainees are from a different generation. Employers, who have been successful in a materialistic world, view their educational and training experience as either being essential (if they had good experiences) or as being disastrous; their views on education and training are usually conservative. Learners are seldom included in decision making about their own course, yet there can be an experiential difference between their background and that of the adults involved in organizing the learning.

There is a basis for discussion between learners, teachers, employers and immediate past learners. Not only do such discussions generate motivation, expectations and objectives but also problems and the assumptions which are relevant for all parties. Details of methods of setting up procedures for such discussions are considered later. However we wish to emphasise that this type of activity is an essential part of each course. Time spent in carrying out the process will reduce alienation and the ensuing motivation will soon enable time to be gained in a formal learning context.

The results of the discussion should be written up as a brief report and a copy held by all those involved with the course, including learners.

It may be that the course members and/or those organizing the course may wish to alter the original agreement as a course progresses, particularly if the course is of considerable duration. Opportunities for the original group members to meet and re-negotiate the agreement should be built into the course. Modification should again be circulated to all involved. There may be constraints on the room for negotiation for externally validated courses, but these do not preclude the process. In order to help learners to identify their needs it may be necessary to provide a mechanism for the group to exchange experiences of learning (see section 1), whether they know one another or not. Those experiences will involve means of coping with assessment and examinations too. The views of each of those involved can be considered in a circle of activity (see figure 2.1)

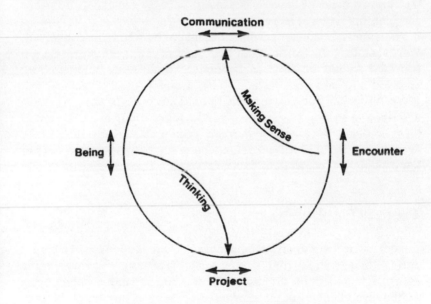

Figure 2.1 Cycle of evaluating

All learners start with themselves and all their past experiences of life, home, learning, peer group and social pressures. The discussion leading to the course are a form of generation of an individual project. The course is the encounter! The experiences, learning and interpersonal activities lead to continual communication changing the persons being. This may be seen as a useful model for learners to take on more responsibility for their own learning. Their needs evolve from the continuous cycling of the loop.

Later in this section we consider some of the means of collecting information which lead to the identification of needs. We cannot emphasise too strongly that different individuals and different groups will have different needs. Identification of individual and group needs is an essential part of the learning process.

Using information from evaluating

It should be remembered that there must be a purpose for evaluating, for collecting information. In our context, this purpose is likely to be the improvement of teaching/learning, perhaps matching the needs and learning styles of learners to the systems of teaching. Very often the outcome of evaluating will be discussion between those involved: the 'evaluator', the learners and the teachers/organizers. Information collected should be seen as facilitating discussion, helping those involved to share and become more aware of each others needs, perspectives and perceptions. It should encourage what we have described in section 1 as creative and loving learning activities for all those involved. We recognise that this is often not the purpose of many evaluations. Perhaps it is a reason why many evaluations are held in low esteem by those at their focus.

The need for planning and purpose

Whatever the focus or style of evaluating, there is need for it to have a purpose and generally for it to have a plan. These may be very specific or broad. Nebulous ideas will often be focused into more specific plans as the evaluating process progresses. There is no harm in this. Questions to be asked, discussed and born in mind when thinking about and undertaking evaluating include:

- what do we hope to achieve?
- how can the important issues be identified?
- who should be involved in negotiating?
- what may be the effects of evaluating?

- how can communication be maintained?
- how can information be collected and analysed?
- who can best collect and analyse information?
- what are the most applicable sources of information?
- what are the constraints (eg. time, manpower, political)?

It may be useful to draw up a checklist using the above questions as headings and to discuss them with colleagues and learners. (See page 70 for details of checklists and the activities at the end of this section for group activities.)

Processes of evaluating

Many processes which we would place under the broad umbrella of 'evaluating' arise naturally and spontaneously during learning. Examples of such could be:

- the puzzled faces and body language of learners in a workshop who have just been asked by the organizer to undertake some task or other, which indicate that more explanation of the task is needed
- the teacher developing computer aided assessment techniques asks her son to try-out the program whilst she observes and later discusses problems with him
- the mathematician who, in a 'problems class', notices the same learning difficulty for many learners and calls together the whole group for additional discussion and help.

Likewise evaluation at the more formal end of the spectrum could be a planned, highly organized and time consuming evaluation of a new multimedia distance learning package. In this case, the evaluation is likely to be undertaken within a fixed time, possibly aimed at bringing about change. Throughout this book, we suggest evaluating as an on going process.

Planning, methods and outcomes are likely to appear very different in the above sets of examples, but each involves the collection and analysis of information to help make informed judgements about how worthwhile something is. In each case, cultural and sociological value judgements have to be made. In a learning context, each of the processes will have (or at least should have) the improvement of learning as one of its major goals.

Although the examples used above may appear to have a starting and definite ending point, only a snapshot has been taken; in reality we consider that the process of evaluating should be continuous and ongoing, an integral part of the total organization and practice of learning.

Let us consider the teacher developing the computer assisted assessment for use in laboratory clasess. The process may be something like:

1 The teacher spends much time marking multiple choice questions designed to assess competencies, attainments or the mastery of particular skills. Because of the time needed to mark questions, feedback to individual learners is often some time after they have completed their practicals and questions about these. Only then can remedial action be planned between teacher and learner.

2 The 'problem' is discussed with learners and colleagues. Methods used in other parts of the institution, and outside, are observed and evaluated. Needs are analysed.

3 Alternatives are discussed. A specification is drawn up, taking due account of constraints. Computer 'generated' and marked test items are decided upon. Learners will be provided with immediate feedback and results are easily noted for later analysis by the teacher.

4 The teacher evaluates existing systems and decides to purchase and modify one of these. The new system is tested, first at home during development and later within the laboratory. The feedback is provided by learners and colleagues which lead to 'fine-tuning' of the system.

5 The system is used by all learners. As they use it, they are observed and later asked to comment about it.

6 Because the analysis of specific learning difficulties is now easier, it is apparent that certain of the associated laboratory techniques are not being successfully mastered. This forms the starting point of further evaluating.

There are a number of identifiable stages in the above process. In practice these are not likely to have clearly definable boundaries but will blur into each other:

1 An issue (need or problem) arises.

2 The issue is analysed, discussed, thought about. Needs, expectations, and hopes are identified.

3 A way forward is arrived at in the light of information collected from various sources. It is decided to make changes.

4 The changes are implemented.

5 The new technique is monitored closely in use for its effects and effectiveness, thus enabling the changes to be evaluated.

6 The change leads to identification of further issues/problems.

Throughout, importance was placed on negotiating and communicating; keeping those involved informed and seeking their help and advice.

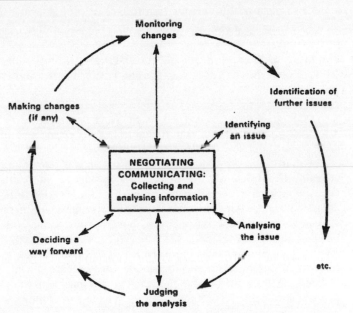

Figure 2.2 Circle of activity

Viewed in this way, the process of evaluating can be considered to be an on-going spiral as shown in figure 2.2. We do not intend this spiral to be prescriptive, but rather to indicate one particular model for evaluating. The model can be applied to many styles of evaluating, but is perhaps most applicable when discussing small scale evaluating, or self-evaluating, as we are concerned with here.

As can be seen from figure 2.2, we considered the collecting and analysing of information to be central to the process of evaluating, therefore the majority of this section is set aside to describe various techniques of collecting information, particularly those most applicable to small-scale processes aimed at helping learners learn. For convenience, we have divided these techniques into: listening and talking; observing; and pencil and paper.

Styles of evaluating

In evaluating, as in most activities, the same 'problem' can be approached from a variety of viewpoints using a variety of approaches. We will not discuss the various theoretical or philosophical assumptions underlying different approaches towards evaluating; the reader interested in this area is directed to the sources noted in the bibliography at the end of this section. Here, we merely indicate four possible approaches to a common problem using a fictitious case study.

> In a certain city, the buses were constantly criticized by the public: they never ran on time and drivers were rude. The bus company decided to call on four expert evaluators to find out what was wrong and to make suggestions about how matters could be improved.
>
> The first evaluator decided that the problem was due to the male chauvinistic attitude of the drivers. He produced an operational description (or hypothesis) of the problem and proceeded to test this definition. He developed an attitude scale comprising a large number of statements on a questionnaire. Questionnaires were handed out to all bus passengers over the period of a week. The evaluator analysed the data using a computer. His report indicated that the problem was not due to a male chauvinistic attitude amongst drivers.
>
> The second evaluator also thought that the problem was due to driver's attitudes. He developed an open-ended questionnaire after consultation with a sample of passengers and drivers. The questionnaire was given to passengers and drivers over a period of a week. Analysis of the questionnaire responses in a report provided some useful pointers to the bus company about how to improve their service.
>
> The third evaluator decided that her area of interest was in the interactions between passengers and drivers. She travelled on many

buses over a long period, talking to passengers and drivers. She also spoke with several members of the management. During early discussions, she identified several issues of importance to those with whom she spoke and used these to devise questions to ask during interviews. A series of short reports were written during the evaluation which formed the focus of discussions between drivers, management and a sample of passengers. The process of evaluating increased communication and helped those people involved to share their experiences and ideas. The final report provided useful information. The bus service was much improved.

The fourth person approached the 'problem' in a different way. He spent each day travelling with one driver, getting to know the driver and many of the passengers very well. Passengers and the driver were encouraged to discuss and explore their feelings, openly sharing their ideas and criticisms. As a result, the driver changed his attitude a great deal, he became very popular with his passengers and an excellent service was provided on his bus. The effects on the overall bus-service was negligible.

Bias of information

Two people describing a particular event will generally provide two different accounts. It is often pointless to think along the lines of 'who is giving the most accurate answer?' or 'who observed the situation correctly?' One of the authors remembers all too well watching, together with a colleague, a video recording of a teacher with a group of learners. Later, both made notes about what was seen, good points, points which could be improved, overall impressions. On comparison, the notes described two very different learning situations. Someone reading these notes without also knowing the context, would be unlikely to realize that they both described the same classroom at the same time seen through the same camera lens!

When collecting information from people, one should remember that what is collected is unlikely to represent an objective reality. Rather, the information represents an individuals' perceptions of reality at the particular time information is collected. Perceptions are likely to depend upon a large number of factors, for example:

- the individuals' view of the 'world'
- the approach adopted to collecting information

- the way in which any questions are asked (or written)
- the rapport between 'supplier' and 'collector'.

Add to this, possible bias or distortion during recording the information ('I hear what I like to hear') and during analysing and summarizing ('I note what I want to note'), and the need for thought and care is obvious.

Approaching the same situation from a number of view points, or using a number of information collectors or techniques generally helps reduce bias. Such approaches are called 'triangulation'. Feeding information back to the person or group who initially supplied it so that they can check and comment upon it is often a valuable technique, even if time consuming. Not only does this reduce bias during recording and summarizing, but also gives the respondent a chance of later reflection upon what he or she said and may increase motivation to take part in future evaluating.

Techniques of evaluating

Listening and talking techniques

If learning is to be a cooperative venture between 'learner' and 'teacher' then there is need for the two groups to have meaningful communication: Such communication is often achieved effectively during discussion between those involved. We wish to emphasise an obvious, but often neglected point: one generally gleans more information by talking with rather than talking to. Therefore 'listening and talking' rather than 'talking and listening'!

Like the majority of information gathering techniques, listening and talking can be organized at a variety of levels and can take many forms. It can:

- be informal or formal
- be non-structured or highly structured
- take place naturally or be specifically organized.

For example, considering individual 'interviews', the spectrum ranges from informal discussion, perhaps better described as a 'conversation with a purpose', to the formal and highly structured interview where the interviewer seeks answers to specific questions. Both approaches, and all those in between have their place: an informal 'chat over a cup of coffee' may well be as valuable as a highly organized and structured set of formal interviews.

We have divided listening and talking techniques into: informal discussions (one to one or groups); one to one interviews; and group discussions. Each has its own particular uses, advantages and disadvantages. As always when evaluating, it is important that the technique and approach adopted is chosen paying due regard to needs, purposes and the context of the particular situation.

Informal discussions

Informal discussion frequently arises naturally and spontaneously, but may also be planned, perhaps at the level of 'drop in for a cup of coffee and a chat'. Such discussions may have no pre-conceived focus or apparent purpose, but may well lead to the raising of issues or problems, allowing those taking part to air their feelings and ideas in a relaxed and informal atmosphere. Discussions can be 'sharpened' or focused as they progress.

Although often considered a tool of the 'evaluator', informal discussion with no organizer or 'evaluator' present is most valuable in the context of improving learning. Groups of learners meeting during a coffee break may well discuss their learning. Much good can be done, both facilitating group cohesion and raising issues of real relevance to the group. On the more negative side, discussions may degenerate into little more than 'shouting' sessions or ones of personal rhetoric.

A skilled and sensitive 'interviewer' can collect much valuable information in informal discussions. The method is often a good starting point in collecting information, whether it be about planning new learning, discussing learning in progress, or reflecting upon that which has taken place. Ideas and issues raised may well form the basis of further investigation.

Individual interviews

We use the term 'interview' to indicate a method which is definitely planned by someone who has a purpose in collecting information. Interviews may be structured, partially structured or non-structured. Some ways of recording information during interviews are noted on page 57.

Structured interviews

Structured interviews involve the interviewer asking specific pre-defined questions. These questions should be carefully planned and written. They often require yes-no, or very brief answers. The interviewer usually has a checklist of questions on which the answers are recorded (see page 70).

Although used frequently for some purposes (eg. market research), structured interviews which allow little latitude for the respondent are of limited use as a technique of collecting information in the context of this book. Where straightforward factual information which requires little thought is required, then questionnaires are often the most applicable method, particularly if there are a large number of respondents. (Further details about questionnaires are given on page 64.) However interviews which use structured questions as starting points for later elaboration are most appropriate.

Partially structured interviews

Partially structured interviews allow the respondent more freedom and latitude than structured interviews. The interviewer is likely to have an interview schedule or check list of questions and issues they wish raised. These are used during the interview to generate discussion, and should be viewed as facilitating rather than inhibiting response.

Partially structured interviews are a very useful technique of information collecting in the context of improving learning. They take advantage of the flexibility of non-structured techniques, while being easier for the interviewer to maintain the desired focus.

New staff in an institute of higher education attend an 'induction course'. Formal evaluating of the effectiveness of the course is undertaken part way through and at the end. Results from these help inform changes to the present course and help in the design of future courses.

One technique used to collect information is the partially structured interview. A schedule of issues to be raised during interviews is drawn up in consultation with the learners and the staff who teach the course. These issues range from the broad and open (eg. 'Do you consider that the course has been useful to you?') to the more specific (eg. 'How long have you spent discussing teaching with your Head of Department?'). The latter type of question generates far more information than that specifically asked for.

During the interview, information is recorded using patterned notes. Information is used to generate a summary for each person interviewed.

Summaries are checked by the respondent for accuracy and further comment before being synthesized into a short written report.

Partially structured interviews need to be planned carefully before the interview. Planning is likely to involve:

- deciding on the issues to be raised

- deciding how to record information

- writing questions and follow-up probes

- trying out questions and probes on a few people from a group similar to those you are planning to interview

- rewriting any questions which are ambiguous, difficult to answer or do not appear to provide what is being asked for.

Non-structured interviews

As distinct from what we have called 'informal discussions', non-structured interviews are carefully planned, have a definite purpose (this could be broad or very specific) and should be undertaken by someone who has practice and skill in the technique. Used with skill, non-structured interviews can yield information which may not emerge by use of other methods. The interviewer can respond to aspects raised by the respondent, and probe these in depth, often returning to them from a different perspective. This approach to collecting information should not be undertaken lightly. A person with little experience of interviewing is best advised to use a more structured technique. As experience and confidence is gained then often movement towards less structured approaches is possible.

Group discussions

Group discussions have a number of advantages and disadvantages compared with one to one interviews. Advantages include:

- the possibility of obtaining information from more people in less time

- group interaction which may encourage individuals to feed-off and build upon each others comments.

A group discussion organized by an experienced and skilful person may help certain more reticent individuals to participate and give more than they would otherwise do.

Potential disadvantages include:

- a possible inhibiting effect upon some individuals, particularly if the discussion is conducted in a less than skilful manner

- over-dominance by the more vociferous or articulate members of the group, leading the direction of discussion and inhibiting contributions by others

- the ease with which focus may be lost.

As noted in the introduction, group discussions may be organized in a non-structured or in a structured way. Non-structured group discussions have an important role, particularly in the early stages of identifying thoughts of the group concerned. However this approach may lead to vague and unfocused discussion and may be an inefficient technique of collecting information in the later stages of evaluating. Once again, when planning a group discussion, we stress the need to consider carefully the purposes and aims of the exercise. (See page 42.) For example, if it is considered important to reduce the effects of the last two disadvantages noted above, then certain structuring techniques described below are useful.

Whatever form the group discussion takes, it is usually necessary to initiate it in some way. However, there may be times when group discussion arises naturally and spontaneously; these may be most fruitful! Some ways of initiating a group discussion include:

- group members can be asked a question

- a problem can be posed to the group

- the leader can introduce the main issues and chair the ensuing discussion; issues may be broad or very specific

- examples, or case studies, can be presented for the group to discuss. Presentation may be verbal, visual or using written documents, perhaps distributed prior to the meeting. A video recording of the group in a learning situation could be shown

- one of the structuring techniques described below may be used.

Structuring discussion using the snowball technique
In essence, snowballing involves individuals personally focusing upon specific issues. Thoughts about these are first shared with small groups and later the whole group. The technique facilitates the maintenance of focus upon specific issues, encourages each member of the group to be actively involved, while also allowing open discussion and interaction.

An example of the use of the technique is given below.

1 All members of the group are asked to write comments in response to a question or issue. The question or issue may be presented verbally or could be written, perhaps in the form of an open questionnaire. Whilst individuals are working, the organizer does a rough count to decide how to put together pairs and later fours. If numbers do not divide, it may be necessary to use 'threes' and 'fives' etc.

2 Individuals form pairs to discuss and look for differences in their comments. As individuals appear to finish their notes (perhaps after 5 minutes or so), the organizer persuades the prospective partner to finish, and to join together to discuss each other's notes. If pairs do not know each other, they can be asked to introduce themselves.

3 Pairs join to form fours for further discussion. Once again, when pairs appear to be finishing their discussions (perhaps after 5 or 10 minutes), the organizer uses the same process to bring together groups of four asking them to look for consensus and possibly differences in what they have written and discussed previously. Groups may be asked to change direction at this stage and should be asked to nominate a rapporteur/spokesperson for later feedback.

4 When one group appears to have finished discussions (perhaps after 10-15 minutes) the organizer goes around all groups asking them to be ready to report back in 5 minutes. It is worth having a small extra activity available for groups who finish early.

5 Each group of four presents its findings to the whole group. The organizer may ask each group in turn for one comment only. These are recorded for all to see. When no further comments are forthcoming, the group may discuss, synthesize and evaluate findings.

As an alternative, snowballing may be organized by allotting the complete group specific times for each of the phases. Although possibly being easier to organize and 'control', keeping the group together tends to lose spontaneity and an individual approach to the work.

There are often advantages in moving-on to the next activity just before group members complete the current activity. In this way, momentum and focus are better maintained.

Information may be recorded by the techniques noted on page 57. Use may also be made of the notes written by individuals in the first part of the exercise and by groups in later parts.

Structuring discussion using the nominal group technique
Nominal group technique (NGT) is a variation of snowballing and
retains similar advantages. A typical NGT procedure is as follows:

1 The group leader identifies a question, or issue, designed to clearly delineate
the scope of the inquiry yet giving individuals sufficient freedom for their
own answers or suggestions.

2 Individuals write their own responses. Cards could be used which may later
be collected by the group leader.

3 If cards were used to record individuals comments, these can be displayed
for the group to read, or may be copied on to acetate, flip chart or board.
Alternatively, the group leader may ask each person in turn to supply one
answer or comment. The process is repeated until no further comments are
forthcoming. Comments are noted by the group leader for all to see. At this
stage no discussion is allowed.

4 Under the direction of the group leader, comments are classified and
synthesized by the group. Discussion should help clarify meanings and
establish the reasons for inclusion in the list. If information is of a more
quantifiable nature, the group may be asked to rank issues in order of
importance.

5 The group leader may encourage final discussion about the issues raised.

Structuring discussion by brainstorming
Brainstorming is a useful way of generating a range of ideas relatively
quickly from a group of about 10-20 members. Organized sensitively,
it overcomes some of the potential problems noted on page 52.

The group (or sub-groups within the whole) are asked a question or
presented with a specific issue or problem. Each member is encouraged to give a short and spontaneous response irrespective of how far-
fetched it is. Responses are recorded by the organizer. At this stage no
discussion is allowed so as not to discourage novel and unusual ideas
and comments. When no further responses are forthcoming, suggestions are discussed, synthesized and evaluated by the group. The key
factors in a brainstorming session are:

1 The initial question or issue; it should be presented in a lively and clear way
to help 'warm-up' the group.

2 The group's initial responses; a 'free-wheeling' approach should be adapted; the group should be encouraged to let go of inhibitions and barriers.

3 Suspend judgement; during the initial response, analysis and evaluation should not be allowed.

4 Cross fertilization; during the brainstorming, group members are likely to feed-off and develop each others responses.

5 Final discussion; allows synthesis and evaluation of ideas generated.

Structuring discussion using buzz groups

A buzz group comprises some two to four people discussing a question or a specific issue for a short period of time. It is a useful technique to focus the attention of each group member and allow each to contribute prior to a more general discussion. Discussion in buzz groups should be kept short. It may be appropriate for the complete group to form buzz groups several times during a group meeting, say at the start of considering each new issue.

The following case study summarizes an approach to evaluating using listening and talking techniques.

The overall goal of the evaluation described here was to collect information from two cohorts of students as part of a course evaluation.

Initial meetings between the 'evaluator' (in this case a member of staff from outside the department responsible for the course) and course, tutors were held to discuss aspects such as:

- the aims of the evaluation

- constraints involved

- the audience for the findings

- practicalities, such as times when students could reasonably be contacted

- an overall plan for the evaluation, particularly for collecting information from students.

Information collected from students was to be used to inform discussion at the course committee about improvements and changes desirable, and also to form part of the overall yearly evaluation of the course.

Constraints which were taken into account included:

- limited time to undertake the collection of information
- a large number of students
- difficulty in assembling all students in one place at one time.

As this was the first time such an evaluation had been undertaken for the particular course, it was considered that students should be given freedom to raise issues of personal importance, therefore initial phases of the process were open, with progressive focusing during later phases.

Information collected was to be synthesized into a written report to be discussed at the course committee: a mixture of staff responsible for teaching on the course and student representatives. The final plan is outlined below.

1 The evaluator met student representatives from each cohort separately. Meetings would best be described as 'informal non-structured discussions' the aim being for the evaluator to allow students the freedom of raising issues of relevance to them. The only prompting necessary to initiate discussion was an overview of the purposes of the evaluation followed by an open question 'what do you think are the good and not so good aspects of your course?'

An hour's open discussion with each group of students led to the identification of a number of issues, summarized and synthesized by the evaluator at the end of discussion.

2 Issues identified during initial discussions formed the basis of a series of open questions on one side of paper. Questions were checked for clarity and understanding by discussion with a small sample of students and course tutors.

3 A letter sent to each student on the course outlined the aims and organization of the evaluation and prompted them to give some thought to the issues previously identified.

4 Students met in groups of approximately 30. These meetings were structured using snowballing, open questions on paper forming the initial (individual) activity. After pairs had discussed the responses, groups of four were asked to identify consensus of opinion about each of the issues. Such consensuses were recorded on another (coloured) sheet of open questions. In this way a record of both individuals', and small group, responses was obtained for later analysis.

5 Each group of four was asked to feedback a comment to the whole group. Comments were recorded on acetate film so that the students could see them immediately and they could be easily be taken away for later analysis.

6 Finally, open discussion was encouraged, once again the main points being recorded on acetate, using a patterned type note. When a new issue was raised by the students, buzz groups were formed to focus initial thoughts.

Recording information from listening and talking

It is relatively easy to record information arising out of a highly structured interview where the respondent answers simple pre-defined questions. An open conversation is less easy to record. In terms of work and amount of time, structured techniques generally require more in the preparation stages where as unstructured techniques require more during analysis.

When recording information, it is important to remember the ease with which data can be biased or distorted, often unconsciously. It is so easy to hear what one wants or expects to hear, or to forget the not so desirable points made. Objectivity can be aided by:

- having more than one person recording information
- discussing the recorded information with the respondents
- triangulation techniques (see page 71).

Note taking

This is perhaps the most obvious technique for recording. Although practice and experience are vital, note taking by one or more people present is applicable to a wide range of situations. If more than one person takes notes, later comparison is possible: we all have a tendency to hear what pleases us!

It may be possible to note only key words and phrases during the 'interview'. These could later be expanded, perhaps being given to those participating for their comment.

Some people find patterned notes (as used in the contents lists of this book) an appropriate way of recording information, particularly in an unstructured situation where the same topic may be returned to several times.

In group discussions, it may be appropriate to make notes on overhead projector acetate, both allowing the group to see comments and also the group leader to easily take comments away for analysis.

Checklists

Pre-prepared checklists can be used during interviews and discussions. They provide a quick and easy way of recording information, while at the same time providing a series of reminders or prompts to the person organizing the session.

Checklists and notes may usefully be combined; checklist to record initial responses and comments, notes to record more detailed or open comments. (See page 70 for further details about checklists.)

Audio recording

Audio recording provides the possibility of providing a complete record of what was said during an interview or conversation. It may however inhibit some individuals and may raise greater questions of confidentiality. Transcription of the tape also takes a great deal of time and is often a boring task.

It may be possible to record parts of discussions (say a summary) whilst using other techniques at other times. As always, care is needed to reduce the possibility of consciously or unconsciously biasing or distorting information. An extreme case known to the authors involved one person audio recording a committee meeting. When the 'transcript' was received it was noted by others present at the meeting to only include certain rather biased information. Needless to say, the full recording had been 'inadvertently' erased!

In addition to a valuable technique of recording information, audio recording is often useful to the organizer of the session in improving their organisational skills.

Observation

Observation is something the majority of us spend much time doing. As was noted earlier, teachers take notice of events while teaching and may modify what they do in the light of what they see. A room full of puzzled faces and certain body language indicates to the teacher that further explanation is needed. Learners working in a small group situation observe one another, make assumptions, take decisions about specific rolls, abilities, motivations etc.

There are times when a more planned and systematic approach to observation may be necessary. Working within a particular environment for a period of time, the observer may become so familiar that they subconsciously become selective in what is seen. By making observation more systematic it is often easier to focus on particular aspects and to collect information pertinent to these. Observation is only one of a range of methods of collecting information. It may well be used in conjunction with other techniques, for example observation combined with listening and talking is often a useful and powerful method of collecting information about what goes on inside 'classrooms'.

Styles of observation

Like all methods of collecting information, there is a spectrum of styles of observing, from the non-structured to the highly structured, from the observer being a participant in the activity being observed, to the observer being an 'outsider' or even a video camera. The style adopted will to an extent control the information collected. This is more likely to be a 'problem' with observation than with many other information collecting techniques.

Non-structured (open) observation
Non-structured or 'open' observation, like non-structured interviews considered earlier, allows the collection of a rich variety of information. It is the technique of many social anthropologists. If the observer enters with as open a mind as possible, things may be seen and recorded which could be missed in a more structured or closed situation. However, practice and skill are needed by the observer in drawing on his or her experience and judgement to focus upon, and record, events considered to be important. It must be realised that however experienced the observer, only a fraction of the interactions and events occurring will be 'seen' and recorded. For this reason, it is often valuable to progressively focus upon certain aspects of particular interest.

Focussing could involve observing people in greater depth (eg. the teacher's interaction with a small group of learners, or the activities engaged by one learner or teacher over a period of time: tracking) or looking only for particular aspects of the learning situation (eg. the way the teacher organizes small group activities). When focusing upon specific aspects, observation may continue to be open or some degree of structuring may be employed.

As part of evaluating to help a newly appointed teacher improve their teaching techniques, a colleague (themselves only recently appointed) observes a series of sessions over a period of time. Although the broad aim is to help learners learn, initially no specific aspects are looked for.

The observer watches a number of sessions with one group of learners, including formal lectures, group work and practicals. Field notes are kept of things which seem interesting. After each observation, the two meet and discuss, using the notes as prompts. It becomes clear that the organization of groups create problems for the learners, and the observer progressively focuses upon this aspect. Groups are observed in turn and the observer starts to discuss with learners their feelings and problems. Information collected is used to discuss alternatives with the teacher who decides to try a range of different approaches. The observer (now focused upon the organization of group work and using listening and talking techniques in addition to observation) continues to report back to the teacher on apparent successes and failures of various styles of group work.

Structuring observation

By structuring observation it is possible to maintain focus upon particular aspects; also the job of observing and recording information may well be made easier. Very often (and particularly in the context of observing for the purposes of improving learning) observation will start in a non-structured way and when issues of importance have been identified, some structuring will be valuable. Structuring can be employed at various levels, from the closed and pre-ordained categories of a commercially available observation schedule, through the observation schedule developed by the observer, to a simple checklist of items to look for and record.

In the context of this book, it is less-likely that a highly structured closed observation schedule where specific behaviours are looked for and recorded at frequent intervals will be used. However there may be some occasions when, for example, it is valuable to have accurate records of the types of questions asked by or the amount of the time the teacher spends interacting with the learners, giving instructions, asking questions, giving information etc. In such cases, an observation schedule of the type shown on page 61 may be valuable.

A checklist is often a simple way of helping the observer structure their observation and record information. An example of a checklist designed to be used during observation of teaching/learning is shown below. It is intended to be used by an 'outside' observer, but could equally be used by the teacher or by one or more of the learners. In practice, greater space is left for written comments:

● Aims of lesson

Time in minutes

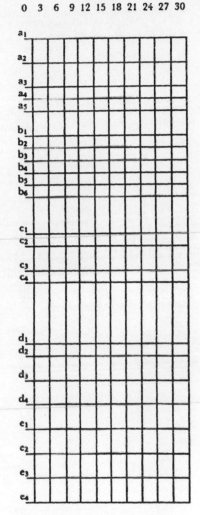

1 TEACHER TALK

1a *Teacher asks questions which are answered by:*
a₁ recalling facts and principles — a_1
a₂ applying facts and principles to
   problem-solving — a_2
a₃ making hypotheses or inferences from
   data — a_3
a₄ designing of experimental procedure — a_4
a₅ observation or interpretation of data — a_5

1b *Teacher makes statements:*
b₁ of fact and principle — b_1
b₂ of problems — b_2
b₃ of hypothesis or speculation — b_3
b₄ of experimental procedure — b_4
b₅ of praise — b_5
b₆ of criticism — b_6

1c *Teacher directs pupils to sources of information
    to:*
c₁ acquire or confirm facts or principles — c_1
c₂ identify or solve problems — c_2
c₃ make inferences, formulation or test
   hypotheses — c_3
c₄ seek guidance on experimental procedure — c_4

**2 TALK AND ACTIVITY INITIATED
AND/OR MAINTAINED BY PUPILS**

2d *Pupils seek information or consult for the pur-
    pose of:*
d₁ acquiring or confirming facts or principles — d_1
d₂ identifying or solving problems — d_2
d₃ making inferences, formulating or testing
   hypotheses — d_3
d₄ seeking guidance on experimental
   procedure — d_4

2e *Pupils refer to teacher for the purpose of:*
e₁ acquiring or confirming facts or principles — e_1
e₂ seeking guidance when identifying or
   solving problems — e_2
e₃ seeking guidance when making inferences
   or testing hypotheses — e_3
e₄ seeking guidance on experimental
   procedure — e_4

The above observation schedule (adapted from *A Science Teaching Observation Schedule* by J. Eggleston *et al.*) is designed to record talk by teachers and pupils. Each time talk which corresponds to a particular category is observed, a tick is placed in the appropriate box.

- Environment
- Use of student's previous knowledge
- Organization of lesson
- Pacing of lesson
- Clarity of information
- Use of aids
- Attitude to learners
- Learner's participation
- Learner's feedback
- Variety and level of questions: to learners; from learners.

The headings allow the observer some flexibility whilst still maintaining focus. Comments written on the check-list form a useful starting point for discussions about the various aspects observed, between the observer, the teacher and (hopefully) the learners. A principle aim here is that of improving understanding and increasing awareness about what happened during a lesson; the observer may well have as much to learn as the teacher!

Recording information from observations

Information may be recorded by a variety of methods including:

- field notes
- observation schedules or checklists
- audio recording
- video recording.

These could be used alone, or in combination.

Field notes
Field notes, either linear or patterned, allow the observer a great deal of freedom and latitude. What appears to be happening, together with comments or prompts for later discussion, can be recorded whilst observing. With practice, field notes can be most effective, but it must always be remembered that no record will be absolute or objective however well intentioned or careful the writer. Analysis of field notes can take time; one useful technique is to use a checklist of headings under which to summarize information.

Observation schedules or checklists

The types of schedules and checklists described earlier, aid the recording and analysing of information and can form a useful starting point for later discussion. Even when using a pre-ordained check list, it is still possible for the observer to make additional notes.

Audio and video recording

Audio and video recording can provide a comprehensive record of events as recorded through the microphone or camera lens. Unlike other techniques, they allow replay for observation, analysis and comment, perhaps by those who were earlier recorded, and are not as prone to bias of information. However, the presence of audio or video equipment is likely to disturb the natural pattern of behaviour and the camera or microphone will record only those events which they have been set-up to monitor. For these reasons, care needs to be taken in their use and in the interpretation of recorded information. It is recommended that the advice of someone knowledgeable in audio and/or video techniques be sought.

Audio recording can provide a complete record of verbal information and is therefore most appropriate where verbal interaction is the focus. It is often difficult to identify the various people recorded on tape, replaying the tape to the group may help. It may be necessary to use more than one microphone, and where much movement is involved, one or more radio-microphones may be necessary.

Video recording has the advantage of providing both audio and visual records and is a most powerful method of providing feedback to those recorded, perhaps being used to initiate group discussion (see page 000).

Pencil and paper techniques

There are many information-collecting techniques that involve the use of pencil and paper, ranging form casual notes to formal examinations. below, we describe a range of such techniques aimed at collecting evaluative feedback from learners and teachers.

Like all evaluation tools, the techniques described here should be used as part of a planned exercise, and should be chosen paying due regard to purposes and alternatives. (See the introduction of this section for further details).

Using results of assessments

Assessments can be used to provide valuable information about the learner's learning, the teacher's teaching and the resources used. All too often, both learners and teachers view assessment as an end point in learning and not as a means of facilitating or improving learning. As discussed throughout the book, we contend that assessment should be an integral and enabling part of the learning process. It should be of value to both learners and teachers in matching their needs.

Analysis of the results of assessments, by both learners and teachers, very often forms the starting point for looking in more detail at a particular problem or issue about learning. This can then be investigated further using techniques described elsewhere in this section.

The use of assessments as an evaluative tool is considered in more detail in Secion 3 where it is discussed in terms of diagnosing learning and teaching.

Questionnaires

A questionnaire is a collection of written questions which are generally answered in the absence of the person who is collecting the information. Whereas most people would recognise that successful interviewing requires skill and experience, many consider that writing a questionnaire is an easy task. This is not so: it is all too easy to produce a questionnaire where questions are ambiguous, instructions unclear, layout poor or information difficult to later analyse. As always, the purposes of using a questionnaire, and the likely uses of collected information should be discussed and clarified.

Use of questionnaires

Questionnaires can collect information quickly from a large number of people, particularly when compared with one-to-one interviews. However where information to be collected is complex, value laden or where in-depth probing of responses is required, questionnaires are of less applicability than listening and talking techniques.

It may be that a questionnaire is the only feasible way of collecting information in certain circumstances: for example distance learning courses where very large numbers are involved or where respondents wish to remain anonymous.

A questionnaire may well be used in conjunction with other information collecting techniques. For example one may be used at the start of snowballing (see page 52) or to collect information from a large number of learners after important issues have been identified during group meetings (see page 51).

Types of questions
Questions may be either open-ended or closed, allowing the respondent some latitude or very little.

	yes no
1 Did you find the workshop useful?	[] []

	very not
2 How useful did you find the workshop?	[] [] [] [] []

3 How useful did you find the workshop?

4 What were your reactions to the workshop?

Questions 1 and 2 are examples of closed questions whereas question 3 is more open-ended. Although basically asking the same question, the information received from the above is likely to be different for each question. Answers to question 4 are likely to display the most variation, depending upon:

● time made available

● space given on the questionnaire

● motivation of the person answering

● the number of respondents.

The choice between using open or closed questions depends upon what information is required, the audience, and the time available to write, answer and analyse the questionnaire. Open-ended questions are quicker and easier to write than closed questions, but the resulting answers are more difficult and time-consuming to summarize. This may be an important consideration where large numbers are involved. Closed questions are often considered easy to answer, but many people become frustrated because they consider the choice of answers does not exactly fit their situation.

Open-ended questions allow the respondents more freedom in the way they answer and in what information they give. For this reason they can often collect information which would not be obtained with closed questions.

It may be advantageous to include both open and closed questions in the same questionnaire to allow people to expand answers and express opinions as well as providing specific information.

If closed questions are presented first, the people completing the questionnaire will have their attention drawn to certain points and this may affect their answers to the questions which follow. If open questions precede closed questions, the respondents are given freedom to express themselves before having their ideas focused by the questionnaire writer. A particularly useful combination for evaluation purposes is a closed question followed by an open one allowing the respondent to qualify his or her answer:

	very				not
5a How useful did you find the workshop?	[]	[]	[]	[]	[]

5b How could it be made more useful for you?

Planning and developing a questionnaire
A questionnaire may be used alone, or may be one of several techniques used to collect information. However it is used, it needs to be planned and written with thought and care. Some initial questions to ask when planning to collect information are given on page 42. If it is decided to use a questionnaire, then the procedure for developing it may be:

1 Decide on the information needed, therefore on the content of the questionnaire.

2 Explore alternative types and sequences of questions (eg. open, closed, use of different wording) and produce a first draft of the questionnaire.

3 Try out the questions on a small sample, preferably people similar to those who will ultimately answer the questionnaire.

4 Redraft and edit in light of the trials.

These stages could form the basis of a checklist as discussed on page 70.

When actually writing the questionnaire, remember that the aim is to obtain the information you want and that which the respondent wishes to give. The questionnaire should encourage those who are answering to do so easily and accurately. The following guidelines may help:

- questions and instructions should be easy to understand for the intended users, be kept as short as possible and be unambiguous

- each question should deal with a single specific point

- questions should not contain double negatives

- questions and instructions should not show bias, lead the respondent towards a particular answer, or be objectionable in any way

- the sequencing of questions should help motivate the respondent (eg. start with easy to answer questions)

- the layout of the questionnaire should be chosen to aid the respondent and should help later analysis (eg. do not cramp questions, keep a consistent layout, leave adequate space between questions and for answers).

Analysing and using information from questionnaires

The analysis of information given on questionnaires may consist of counting and tabulating numeric answers and summarizing open questions. If a computer is available this could be used, allowing quicker and possibly more sophisticated analysis particularly where large numbers are involved. Numerical information presented graphically is often a very useful form.

Information from questionnaires may be summarized and displayed on summary sheets or checklists. It is useful to consider the layout of these sheets when writing the questionnaire. For closed questions, it may be possible to use a blank questionnaire form as a summary sheet, noting by each question the overall answers to that question. For open questions, summary cards may be useful. Each time a new idea or comment is noted this is written on a card. If the same (or very similar) response is noted on another questionnaire, this is recorded by tallying the card corresponding to the comment. In this way, the set of cards summarizes responses and their frequency for each question.

Delphi procedure

The Delphi procedure is a systematic way of collecting and combining ideas from a number of individuals. While encouraging a consensus of opinion, it also enables divergences from this consensus to be identified and recorded. Briefly, the method involves collecting information which is later analysed and fed back to the members of the group to elicit new information which is subsequently analysed and fed back. It therefore comprises a number of cycles of activity.

Initially used as a way of obtaining predictions from 'world experts', the Delphi procedure is often a valuable way of collecting evaluative information. However due to the iterative nature of the technique, it can be very time consuming for the organizer.

Those taking part do not need to come into contact. Information can be collected by questionnaire (see page 64) and fed back by short written reports (or use can be made of audioconferencing). Alternatively, individual interviews may be used if appropriate.

A typical Delphi procedure could involve the following:

1 Information about a specific issue is collected from the group.

2 The organizer collates, analyses and summarizes this information. If for example a closed questionnaire has been used, then the summary may show numbers of responses to each item. If more open techniques have been utilized (eg. semi-structured interviews) the summary may be a short written report.

3 Information contained within the summary is fed back to the group for their

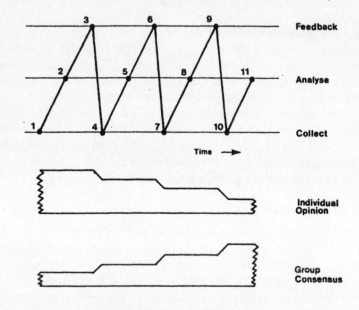

Figure 2.3 *Delphi cycles*

consideration. This is likely to prompt a further set of comments. At this stage, participants are asked to consider their ideas in light of the overall group response. In this way, individuals with only weak convictions are likely to move towards the group norm, while those with strong feelings will maintain and justify their views.

4 Information generated from stage 3 is collected, and so the process continues as shown in figure 2.3.

Diaries

Diaries are written records of events noted from the perspective of the writer or writers. They can range from brief notes completed on a pro-forma or logsheet, to long and deeply insightful personal reports of events. Diaries are often most appropriate for building up a regular record of events over a period of time, such as events occurring within a group of students, or during the development of curriculum materials. They form a very useful method of monitoring learning during project type work.

Year tutors in a large secondary school felt unable to teach satisfactorily due to frequent interruptions from students and other staff. As part of a larger evaluation intended to inform decisions about restructuring of the timetable, year tutors were asked to keep a simple diary over a period of four weeks recording details of who consulted them, when, the time taken, the nature of the consultation and the priority they attached to the consultation. A pro-forma was designed for this purpose.

Analysis of the diaries indicated trends regarding the most busy times for tutors of each year group, the types of consultation at different times and the priority attached to different reasons for consultation. As a result, the school was able to restructure the year tutor's teaching to allow them to be free when most needed, and to include specific times for the tutor to meet their year group for discussion, trouble shooting and to give administrative information. The latter was found a particularly valuable and efficient use of time by both students and staff, and formed the focus of a later evaluation.

During an audio-visual aids assignment, learners are asked to keep an accurate diary of events. This is intended to serve two main purposes:

- It helps the learners focus upon what they are doing, why they are doing it and enables them to, reflect on their successes and failures!

- It provides a valuable record for the teacher during discussion with the learners, as much work is undertaken at a distance from the tutor.

Date	Activity, problem, plan etc.	Location	Time spent	Material or equipment used

Checklists

Simple checklists are often a useful aid when collecting, recording and summarizing information. They are straightforward to write, easy to complete and help maintain focus. For example the questions noted on page 42 could form the basis of a checklist to be used by a group planning to evaluate as shown below. Answers to each question can be completed either by individuals or by the whole group working together.

When developing a technique of collecting information, a checklist could be used to ensure that each stage and aspect of the planning has been considered.

A group designed the checklist below to help them maintain focus during the development of a questionnaire. (The list given on pages 66–7 was used as the basis of this checklist).

1 The general area of interest.

2 Specific content areas

3 The target group (age, any particular characteristics etc.)

4 Is a questionnaire the most appropriate way of collecting information.   (If No then stop here!)

5 The most appropriate format:

6 Types of closed question:

7 Later analysis of questionnaires considered?

8 First draft completed?

9 All draft questions and instructions evaluated by:

10 All questions and instructions redrafted?

11 Layout evaluated by:

In addition, a further checklist was produced when evaluating the individual questions. This was based on the guidelines given on page 66.

Triangulation

Triangulation is the process of mapping out and explaining more fully. In an educational and training context the geographical analogy can be extended further. In order to map out part of the countryside certain triangulation points have been established from which others are viewed in three directions. The approach of evaluation from different perspectives is the basis of triangulation. There are potentially five methods of triangulation, some of which are more common than others. The purpose of each is to reduce the distortion produced by evaluating in one context by one method. For example, using a structured questionnaire limits the response that can be made to those questions which are asked. The questionnaire may be deliberately designed to elicit responses in a limited area determined by the originator. Because of the originators' interest and the limitations of response, the questionnaire is likely to be filtering, biasing and distorting. Each method has a similar problem. If that questionnaire is used with one set of learners while their teacher is present a further sampling bias will occur.

The most obvious methods of triangulation in a small-scale context include:

- *Methods triangulation* involving the use of three or more different information collecting techniques (eg. interviews, observations, questionnaire, group discussion). Ideas which occur from two or more techniques have more reliability than those from only one. However if the interview and questionnaire are both structured with a similar structure, similar responses are to be expected! An alternative is to use the same techniques on different occasions which checks for consistency of respondent's view over time.

- *Investigator triangulation* where three or more different investigators or observers are employed. The sharing of perspectives, data and information enables the clarification of interpretations and a critical review of techniques. This sharing and critical reviewing also enables the involvement of learners and teachers in the process, ie. using evaluation for learning.

• *Time triangulation.* Many techniques give a snapshot at one point in time (eg. a questionnaire or an examination). An alternative approach is to track an individual learner over a period of time (a sort of 'cine' approach). A mixture of the cross sectional (snapshot) and longitudinal (cine) approaches again aids confidence in data and information.

The remaining three methods are more difficult to apply in the context of a small-scale self-evaluation.

• *Space triangulation* involves cross cultural or cross sub-cultural investigations. This method can be very illuminating with respect to formal procedures such as structured questionnaires, attitude scales and so on where different cultures may interpret the words and their intention differently (this is particularly so for attitude scales which can be very culturally biased).

• *Levels triangulation* involves using different individuals, groups or collectivities (eg. organizations, societies, cultures). Whilst the variation in techniques suggested earlier may enable this, here, the design of the evaluation would specifically aim at this form of triangulation.

• *Theoretical triangulation* involves different investigators using different or competing theories. One way of presenting this type of triangulation is by using advocates for each theory presenting their case as in a court of law.

While evaluating can be systematic it cannot be compared with a scientific investigation. In the majority of scientific investigations if there are 32 variables, 29 may be kept constant whilst the remaining 3 are investigated. A single method can be chosen which will usually give unambiguous information on the selected phenomena. Human interactions are complex and multi-variate. The techniques used to investigate such interactions are not neutral, they filter and give a selective experience of the environment. When one technique biases and distorts the picture, the data can be an artefact of the technique or of the collector of information. The multi-technique approach will give more confidence, especially if contrasting techniques are used.

A college wished to investigate the attitudes of their day release students to their time in college. The immediate suggestion was an attitude scale to be developed specifically for the purpose. The technique would be convenient to use, provide data in a quantitative form and be easily accessible to critics and employers. However many attitude scales have little or no psychological basis or criteria for design. The scale will probably be culture bound, so ethnic minorities and different socio-economic groups will give different responses. It will probably get different responses on different occasions: so it is time bound. Alternative approaches considered were an in-depth study of individuals over a period of time. Because the study is of individuals it is idiosyncratic while providing insights. In addition such studies are difficult to replicate. Alternative approaches based on these techniques chosen were:

- track individuals and identify key issues as a basis for a questionnaire to all students (see page 64)
- use a questionnaire and track in depth a sample (say very positive, very negative, ethnic minority, high performer, low performer).

Both of these techniques are using time and method triangulation to help reduce bias.

Large-scale evaluations may be able to use multi-methods (eg. teachers' ratings of learners, records of achievement, psychometric data, sociometric data, case studies, observation) and repeat these in several representative organizations.

It should be clear that more objective 'scientific' approaches (eg. normative assessment procedures) give more generalized information and less idiosyncratic information whilst subjective individualized approaches (eg. tracking, case studies) give more idiosyncratic information and less generalizable information. Distortion will tend to occur with the use of only one approach.

One monitoring system sometimes used with qualitative data is a panel of judges. Is it a form of triangulation if all the panel of judges subscribe to the same values? Critics liken the panel of judges to a mystery tour. The passengers on one mystery tour had a sweepstake about their destination, the driver won $48!

A possible routine for an evaluation procedure incorporating triangulation could be:

1 Identify the area of interest / problem; it may be helpful to specify the purposes in detail; it will certainly be necessary to reduce the scope to something which is manageable; identify the expected reporting methods.

2 Identify the setting, the administrative and organisational structure, procedural problems, finance and resources available

3 Identify potential techniques, list possibilities and relate to the information required. Determine from the total picture whether methods are efficient, supportive, unsuitable, identify which are quantifiable and non-quantitative, which use individual responses, which group responses. Determine which techniques are going to be considered most important.

4 Make decisions on the extent and range of information which will meet the original criteria to provide a balanced (triangulation) framework within the resources available.

5 Implement the decisions; devising, piloting techniques then collecting and analysing data.

6 Interpret the data to give information in a suitable form for reporting The triangulation has been built into this process, but it is important to identify the form(s) of triangulation used.

Suggested group activities

1. How do we identify issues of real importance?

Ask the group to either brainstorm or use a snowball technique. Alternatively, one of the group could be asked to describe what led to evaluating in an instance with which they are familiar as a basis for critical review.

2. How can an evaluation be planned and techniques chosen?

What we are about is developing a plan, or strategy for evaluating. We have found a case study approach to be particularly valuable. The case study could be given to the group, or a real example which one or more of the group is familiar with could be used. The whole group could be split into smaller groups (say four or six) who work from guidelines indicating specific tasks. For example, with school teachers the case study may be:

> The geography department, which is part of the humanities sector (comprising careers, economics, geography, history, religious educa-tion and social studies departments), introducing a new series of study packs used for about half of the year, by their fourth year mixed ability students.
>
> After examinations at the end of the year, teachers have begun to express disquiet over the apparent progress of their students. Initial

reaction to the packs which are well illustrated and attractively presented had been favourable. However, it is now being questioned whether or not the new material is providing an effective learning resource.

The group could be asked to read through the first part of section 2 (pages 39–48), discuss the list of questions on page 42 and draw-up a check-list of answers to these. Any group finishing the process early could be asked to start considering techniques in more detail. When all groups have finished, they give a brief report to the whole. The groups may also be asked to evaluate how well they functioned.

3. Developing techniques and instruments for collecting information

Once again, small groups (say four-six) working together generally function more successfully than a large group. This activity could follow from number 2 above, or could be separate. If one or more of the group has a real need, so much the better. We have found several approaches which work well:

- Developing a technique or instrument for a particular purpose (eg. a group discussion to collect particular information). It may be useful to use a checklist to help maintain focus and provide the group with prompts.

- The analysis of 'specimen' instruments. (eg. several questionnaires could be provided for the group to discuss, evaluate and rewrite).

- The use of a case study or situation.

If several groups are involved, then different groups could be asked to use different approaches, reporting and discussing differences later. The relevant parts of this section could be used to provide prompts and focus for the group.

4. What is the utility of evaluating?

Use one of the group discussion techniques noted in this section.

5. Who evaluates the evaluators?

A discussion based around this question will raise many fundamental issues including those of a philosophical and sociological nature.

Difficulties and criticisms

The evaluating that we have described depends heavily on qualitative and indirect methods. The data and information is collected in a semi-structured or non-structured way. The analysis of the data and information is done by an individual or a group. The process of filtering, analysing and reporting is not explicit, whereas structured approaches make more explicit the filtering and bias by the very questions which are used. The more qualitative approaches are open to distortion making them less reliable and open to questions of validity. Continuous communication with all those involved helps overcome these problems.

The qualitative style of evaluating enables the writing of reports which are easy and interesting to read or hear, particularly where participants' quotations are included. However selection of which quotations to use and the ordering of the report are very much in the creative hands of the presenter. That presenter will have personal values (or even axes to grind) and however honest, will tend to bias the report to support their own values. One way of overcoming this problem is for the presenter to start by giving their own views or values so that the report can be judged taking these into account. Again the offering of a draft report for critical review by those involved can provide an opportunity for editing or the incorporation of different views. On several major projects, particularly in the USA, there has been a review of the evidence by a different set of workers who also bring together their conclusions. These conclusions may conflict with those of the original workers. The alternative reports have been published incorporating a discussion between the two sets of workers. This strategy has potential but is obviously time consuming. Another strategy is to use different advocates who present their cases based on the evidence; rather like a court of law.

The reporting often provides the sort of information that is useful to local authorities, funding bodies and employers in order to make judgements. Much current evaluating in institutionalized education and training has moved towards internal procedures using more qualitative and illuminative styles. It is easier to doctor the report to give a rosy picture than it would be with conventional quantitative data. However the use of the report as a means of judging the evaluating process is a 'tail wagging the dog' problem. An advantage of the process is the learning which takes place.

If we focus on the learning process for the institution or the learning system, a rather different picture emerges. The responsibility for part of the evaluating can be with the learner, part can be done co-operatively between teachers and learners. The focus of the process is about improving the potential for learning. The collecting and analysing of data will probably encourage communication which did not occur before. By communicating during the spiral process (see page 45) the learning environment will be changed. Here, the evaluating is not about ensuring that no change takes place before the report is presented but about enabling innovation and change as a collaborative venture of all those involved.

Where evaluating is focused around the objectives or criteria of the course, there are potential difficulties. It is always possible to carry out fine tuning of a course to ensure that criteria are met better and better. However this inward looking approach fails to consider two other important aspects. The criteria may need challenging; who decided on those criteria, why are they relevant in the particular context under review? What other learning is occurring that is not specified by the criteria?

A potential source of information which was only briefly mentioned, are learners who have already completed the course. A representative sample may be difficult to locate. The relevance of criteria may be a case where learners now in the next stage of their development (whether still in formal education or training or in real life situations) will have firm views. The potential for using past learners in association with current learners is considerable if evaluating is seen as a learning process.

Some will see the evaluating as not going far enough along the lines of improving practice by enabling teachers and learners to elicit and modify one another's value systems. These processes require, for example, video recordings of actual learning sessions where teacher and learners explain what they think was happening. The approach can be very threatening to all concerned so should only be used where all parties are in agreement and experienced and sensitive 'evaluators' are involved. It is clearly easier to use where face to face contact occurs rather than distance study.

Finally a further criticism can be made that the assumptions behind a highly structured imposed evaluation such as that used by the first evaluator on the buses (see page 46) is incompatible with an unstructured facilitator (a participant observer such as the fourth evaluator). In our opinion this is not always so; the strategies and styles of evaluating should relate to the problem being investigated rather than being ordered by philosophical dogmatism.

Annotated bibliography

Baker, E L and Atkin, M C (1984)
Formative Evaluation of Instructional Development. In Bass, RK and Dills, CR (eds)
Instructional Development: The State of the Art II
Dubuque, Iowa: Kendall/Hunt.
A good outline of practice in USA covering most of the essential features we have discussed.

Delbecq, A L, Van de Ven, A H and Gustafson, D H (1975)
Group Techniques for Program Planning
Illinois: Scott, Forsman.
Describes in detail the theory and application of the Delphi and nominal group techniques.

Gredler, M (1992)
Designing and Evaluating Games and Simulations: a Process Approach
London: Kogan Page.
Experiential activities, games and simulations are gaining popularity and acceptance. The book analyses process characteristics of activities which facilitate learner actions, the types of actions or behaviours that receive reinforcement, the nature of feedback for the individual's actions and the relationship of the individual to others in the exercise.

Guba, E G and Lincoln, Y S (1989)
Fourth Generation Evaluation
London: Sage.
Fourth generation evaluation represents a monumental shift in evaluation practice. The authors highlight the inherent problems faced by previous generations of evaluators and lay the blame for failure and non-utilization at the feet of the unquestioned reliance on scientific/positivist paradigm of research. Fourth generation evaluation, a more

informed and sophisticated approach, moves beyond scientific approaches to include the myriad of human, political, social, cultural and contextual elements involved in evaluation.

Hamilton, D et al (eds) (1977)
Beyond the Numbers Game
London: Macmillan.
An extremely readable collection of papers on evaluation. Contains a wide range of extracts from most of the eminent evaluators, the central thesis being that evaluation involves far more than measurement of outcomes.

Harlen, W (1978) (ed)
Evaluation and the Teacher's Role
Basingstoke: MacMillan.
A collection of papers dealing with a wide range of evaluation issues, many having a focus of 'evaluation for innovation'.

Harris, N D C, Bell, C D and Carter, J E H (1981)
Signposts for Evaluating: A Resource Pack
London: Council for Educational Technology/Schools Council.
A pack providing basic materials for teachers involved in institutional or classroom evaluation. The pack is in three parts: an introduction to evaluating; techniques for evaluating; some theoretical aspects of evaluating. The techniques elaborated vary from assessment procedures to curriculum analysis, from observation to interviewing.

Harrison, C (1980)
Readability in the Classroom
Cambridge: Cambridge University Press.
A practical guide for teachers for assessing readability and matching notes and books to learners. Specific reference is made to the problems found in various subjects. The main readability formulae are described and assessed, and there is comment on how they can be used when writing material. The book also includes a computer program for assessing readability.

Hartley, J (ed) (1980)
The Psychology of Written Communication (2nd edition)
London: Kogan Page.

A collection of articles addressing issues such as: theoretical aspects of learning, how learners develop writing skills; how to design written information so as to have maximum impact; the use of microfilm, viewdata and computer systems; scientific writing. There is a useful section on the design of written information.

Huczynski, A (1983)
Encyclopaedia of Management Development Methods.
Aldershot: Gower.
Although the title is indicative of a specific audience, it is likely that all educators and trainers will find much of relevance in this book. Some 300 methods of providing learning/teaching situations are outlined, generally with references to sources of more detailed information. In addition, a framework is provided to help teachers choose and analyse methods

Kaufman, R and English, F W (1979)
Needs Assessment: Concept and Application
Englewood Cliffs: Educational Technology Publications.
The book is divided into two sections: concepts and basic models underlying needs assessment to provide a framework for successful application; applications of the most useful models including case studies of needs assessment in education, government, commerce, industry and the armed services.

Keeves, J P (1988)
Educational Research, Methodology and Measurement: An International Handbook
Oxford: Pergamon.
A compendium of the theory and practice of educational research.

Payne, S L (1951)
The Art of Asking Questions
Princeton: Princeton University Press.
Although now an old text, this is still a useful source of information about the importance of the ways in which questions can be asked. Many practical hints and tips are given through the frequent use of examples.

Rowan, J and Reason, P (1981)
Human Inquiry: A Source Book of New Paradigm Research

London: Wiley.
A book outlining involving cooperative and participant approaches.
Figure 2.1 originates from this book.

Shipman, M (1979)
In-School Evaluation
London: Heinemann.
Aims to provide a 'do-it-yourself' manual for evaluating a wide range of curicula and extracurricular activities. These are also applicable outside the school environment. The book describes in plain language various assessment techniques, both internal and external.

Shrock, S A (1984)
Naturalistic Inquiry: an alternative Methodology for Instructional Development Research. In Bass, R K and Dills, C R (eds) *Instructional Development The State of the Art II*
Dubuque, Iowa: Kendall/ Hunt.
The paper considers non-obtrusive means of inquiry whilst dealing with colleagues and clients, rather than the more traditional experimental design using obtrusive methods.

Smyth, J (1990)
Teacher Evaluation as the Technology of Increased Centralism in Education
In Bell, C D (ed) *World Yearbook of Education: 1990. Assessment and Evaluation.*
London: Kogan Page.
Portraying teachers as a much maligned group within the community would not be hard at all given recent 'educational reforms'. The paper argues that teachers need to become more active in deconstructing dominant forms of evaluating and articulating and developing alternative ways of construing and evaluating their own and one another's teaching.

Strachan, R M (ed) (1983)
Guide to Evaluating Methods: A Manual for Microtechnology Innovation
Cambridge: National Extension College.
Although the focus in case studies is on microelectronics innovation, the majority of the text has wider applicability. A brief outline of a

wide range of evaluation techniques is given. These are discussed in the context of improvement of curriculum materials and of learning.

Straughan, R and Wrigley, J (eds) (1980)
Values and Evaluation in Education
London: Harper and Row.
An interesting examination of standards, measurement, assessment, evaluation and values in education. The links between these concepts are explored in depth. The second part of the book looks at the ways in which these concepts arise in different subject areas of the curriculum.

Stubbs, M and Delamont, S (1976)
Explorations in Classroom Observation
Chichester: John Wiley.
Focuses on the study of what happens between learners and teachers, describing (often via case study) methods of observing, recording and analysing interactions. Provides a brief but valuable overview of research into teaching/learning.

Sudman, S and Bradburn, N (1982)
Asking Questions: A Practical Guide to Questionnaire Design
San Fransisco, Jossey Bass.
A detailed text moving from the simple to the complex with a particular emphasis on interpretation and misinterpretation.

Tessmer, M (1993)
Planning and Conducting Formative Evaluations
London: Kogan Page.

Wragg, E C (1979)
Designing and Analysing Interviews: Nottingham University Rediguide II
Maidenhead: TRC Rediguides.
This is a small book which describes uses of interviews, different styles, and some of the pitfalls of interviewing. It is a good starting point for anyone needing straightforward information.

Section 3. Assessing for learning

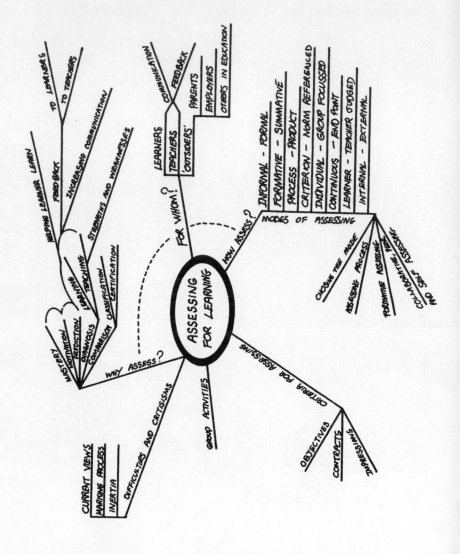

Section 3. Assessing for learning

Section 3. Assessing for learning

Introduction

Assessing of sorts has been with us from the beginnings of recorded history. The Romans used many different types of assessing, and earlier there was Eve with the apple! All indications are that it will remain with us for the foreseeable future at most levels of compulsory and post-compulsory education. Indeed, we are all continually assessing, passing judgement on fellow human beings and inanimate objects. Judgements are based on our own value systems and those prevalent in society. In some situations assessing is made by an 'expert' judge or critic: the art critic, the music critic, the external examiner.

In education and training, two broad aspects form the focus of assessing:

- the learners
- the 'resources' which are assembled to aid learning, including print, media, curricula and the teachers themselves.

Throughout this book we use the term 'assessing' to indicate the former, and 'evaluating' when we are discussing the latter. Although this distinction is commonly made in Britain, in American literature the word 'assessing' is little used in this context; 'evaluating' serving to label both concepts.

In the first part of this section we broadly consider the why? and for whom? of assessing.

Why assess?

Try thinking of reasons why assessing often takes such a key position in education. Better, try to persuade colleagues and/or learners to do the same. (See the activities at the end of this section for one way of organizing such an activity.)

There are many reasons suggested for keeping clear records of learners' progress, for example to help the learner realize what they have learned; to help the teacher plan for future learning or remediation; to meet the requirements of the National Curriculum, National Vocational Qualification, profiles, records of achievement, standardised tests, etc. These records originate from some form of informal or formal assessing organized either by the teacher or by the learner. The recording and discussion of assessing often forms the basis of the main communication between the teacher and the learner. Assessing without communication is of doubtful value: communication between the teacher and the learner is an essential part of the learning process and should be on a regular basis. An obvious problem is that the means of communication may well need to be different for different learners according to their character and preferred styles of learning. The relative roles of teacher and learner are also crucial: in schools where the teacher is more mature, it is easy to become patronizing; in higher and adult education the learner may be more mature. If the communication between teacher and learner is to have any meaning in a motivational or learning context, its aims need to be clear and it needs to be carefully planned and executed. (Some ways of facilitating and evaluating communication are discussed in section 2.)

Another important aspect of the communication is the accessibility of the teacher to the learner. In distance study for example, the only means of communication between the learner and the teacher may be by telephone or mail. It is clear that the style and method of communication and of assessing will be very different in this situation from that where the teacher and the learner have access at any hour of the day, such as in a residential learning environment.

In formal institutionalized education and training, the contact between learner and teacher can be worse than in distance study. For example if the learning is mainly focused around lectures, the teachers may carry such a high teaching load of lectures that no other contact is available to the learners. Although it would be hoped that such an extreme case did not exist, nevertheless the higher the work load for both teachers and learners, the less likely it is that communication and regular assessing will occur which are necessary for both parties to gain the maximum satisfaction in their contact.

When the focus is on small group work, there is no guarantee that there is any better communication and contact, although where the small group work is centred around the development of interpersonal skills it is more likely to occur. The normal way to help communication develop is to allocate personal tutor time for each learner; however this can be counter-productive as the responsibility for the learning is once again being vested in the teacher rather than in the learner. In the long term, each of us needs to take more and more responsibility for our learning in a world where the knowledge base is increasing at a phenomenal rate, let alone the technological developments which give us all more access to information and more difficulty in discriminating between that which is relevant and useful and that which is garbage! Similarly the role of the teacher changes to a guide, facilitator or even a co-traveller rather than a presenter or performer. We return to this in sections 4 and 5.

In the following pages we examine some of the reasons most commonly advocated reasons for assessing learners:

- mastery
- increasing the motivation of learners
- prediction of an individual's potential
- diagnosis of learning
- diagnosis of teaching
- evidence of competence or attainment
- certification, classification and comparison with other learners.

It must not be overlooked that as a part of education, assessing is to a lesser or greater extent, a tool of socialization into a particular society, a political activity which may well be aimed at perpetuating certain values, encouraging change, or maintaining the status quo.

Assessing for motivation

Assessing may increase the motivation of the learner. However, it has other more negative effects such as increasing stress or decreasing the desire to continue studying. The dividing line between motivation and demotivation is a fine and varying one. It is likely to be different for each learner and for a particular learner it will vary from time to time and from situation to situation. These factors must be born in mind by those organizing the assessing and by the learners themselves. The motivational effects of assessing may well be due to different factors, for example the effects of:

● knowing that one is to be assessed

● knowing, or anticipating, the results of assessing

● being actively involved in the process of assessing (eg. as found in some records of achievement).

It would be encouraging to think that these factors go towards increasing the motivation of learners in their learning. But equally the learner who constantly obtains low marks could be discouraged from trying. An assignment out of class, the driving test, the end of unit examination are likely to act as a carrot, or a big stick, depending upon the individual's point of view, the way in which assessing is presented and the actual processes adopted. There is a large difference between the 'motivational' effects due to knowing that one is to be assessed and those due to helpful and constructive feedback about some work.

Throughout the book, we concentrate upon the motivational aspects of assessing and evaluating and discuss ways of using these in order to facilitate learners' learning.

Assessing for prediction

Although only a limited number of assessment tools and techniques are designed with prediction as their aim, many are used in this way. In secondary/high schools, class examinations often form the basis to judge future courses of study. Examinations at 16+ are used to select those learners considered 'suitable' for entry to further courses. Examination results are used as an important factor for selection to employment and particularly for entry to higher education. Likewise in higher education, assessing often forms hurdles over which learners have to jump in order to continue with their chosen course of study or to obtain specific qualifications or credits for employment. In much of technical and commercial training, success at one level opens the possibility of training at a higher level.

In all of these cases, if it is assumed that 'those who score well now will score well later', then assessing is being used as a predictor of future potential. Although often used in this way, many studies have shown that commonly used assessments have little predictive value of an individual's future performance. Even the results of examinations used to select for higher education in a similar subject area rarely indicate a high degree of correlation. A higher correlation with future performance may well be found between the learners motivation, and/ or style of learning, than between traditionally used predictors.

Assessing for diagnosis of learning

Assessing has an important role to play in the diagnosis of learning (that is the identification of learning that has apparently taken place, learning difficulties experienced by individuals or groups, or identification of future learning needs). Used in this way, assessing does not necessarily involve formal tests or measurements and is unlikely to involve comparative grading of learners. Here, we are not discussing diagnostic assessment instruments used by specialists to diagnose particular learning difficulties, but more usual assessments used by teachers and learners in a diagnostic way, focusing upon either individuals or groups. The latter has also much relevance to the diagnosis of possible teaching (or organizational problems) as discussed below.

During teaching, teachers constantly attempt to assess learning: from asking direct questions to receiving non-verbal communications from learners. Likewise, the learners are likely to be constantly assessing themselves, their peers, the environment and their teacher. All help to inform the learners and teacher of their successes and failures in achieving goals, and hopefully aid 'fine tuning' or 'hole patching and plugging' of the learning process. In this area the activities of 'assessing' and 'evaluating' tend to blur into each other. The major aim of assessing used in a diagnostic way is to provide information of use in helping learners learn, the recurrent theme of this book. A crucial element is discussion between learners and between learners and teachers based on the assessing in order to identify difficulties. The attainment targets and competency expectations may provide a framework for diagnostic assessment.

Assessing for diagnosis of teaching

In the previous section we have briefly considered assessing as being focused upon the learning achieved by learners. However, assessing learners may well provide valuable information about the teaching, organization or curriculum to which learners have been subjected. Consider a simple example where learners have answered a number of assessment items producing the simplified results shown in figure 3.1. The items could be formal test questions, project marks or even peer assessing. For simplicity, we have shown numeric 'marks'. Comments, informal assessing and the results of questionnaires could well form the basis for this application.

Assessment Learner	A	B	C	D	E	*Total*
Alison	8	4	7	5	9	*33*
Brian	4	3	7	5	8	*27*
Chris	2	4	6	5	7	*24*
Duncan	8	2	5	4	5	*24*
Elisa	4	1	4	7	6	*22*
Total	*26*	*15*	*29*	*26*	*35*	

Figure 3.1 *Diagnosing teaching through assessment results*

The results may be treated in a number of ways. For comparison of learners, it is most probable that the total marks of each learner would be compared. However in figure 3.1 the total marks for assessment B are lower than totals for other questions/assessments. Is this due to:

- Problems with the assessing itself?

- Lower than average quality of teaching in the area of work to which the assessing relates?

- The majority of learners failing to have studied the work to which the assessing relates?

- Work inappropriate to the learners involved?
- Lack of confidence amongst the learners?
- A different standard of marking for the assessment?

Without further analysis, only a guess could be made, but considered in this way the results of assessing could well lead to a questioning of teaching methods or the appropriateness of the curriculum content. It may form the starting point of more detailed evaluating aimed at improving learning. (Evaluating is considered further in section 2.)

Assessing for competence

There are many aspects of learning which require a demonstration of competence (or mastery) on behalf of the learner. The pharmacist mixing drugs would be short lived in his or her profession if correct quantities were obtained only 85% of the time. The trainee mechanic replacing the parts of an engine would be most unpopular if only three quarters of the parts were correctly assembled! In these cases, assessing is both a valuable and necessary part of the learning process, providing feedback to both the learner and teacher. In general, interest will be on the learner's ability to achieve the desired result (a correctly mixed drug or an engine which works) rather than upon comparing one learner with another.

In the examples used above, the focus of assessing is on the attainment or non-attainment of specific skills. It is likely that importance is attached to demonstration of competence and if a particular learner takes longer than average to achieve it, this will be considered acceptable. The tendency is towards 'fixed learning, variable time' rather than the more normally found 'fixed time, variable learning'.

Assessing for certification, classification and comparison

We have chosen to group together certification, classification and comparison not because they must be inextricably related, but because in practice the dividing lines are often very blurred.

It can be argued that much assessing currently practiced in education has certification, classification or comparison as one of its major aims. The learner is tested in relation to other learners and to the values, competencies and attainments ascribed by society. Results of such assessing are used to rank and select, allowing employers and the education system to choose.

In this book, we do not concentrate upon these end-point purposes of assessing. However current trends towards competencies and attainments tend to blur the boundaries. Those wishing further details are referred to the bibliography at the end of this section.

Assessing for whom?

There are inextricable relationships between the purposes of assessing and their intended audiences. Taking an extreme example an assessment tool intended to highlight teaching difficulties would be of little use in providing information of value to a future employer about the achievements of an individual applicant. However there are many instances where assessing can have a variety of purposes, for example it may be used to provide information to the learner about their strengths and weaknesses whilst at the same time providing information to the teacher of a 'hole plugging and patching' nature.

In earlier parts of the text we have suggested that possible audiences for the 'results' of assessing are: the learners, the teachers and other 'outsiders' (eg potential employers, teachers in other institutions).

Assessing for the learners

Rarely is assessing organized with the learners as the main audience for the results. Yet if assessing is to be a real aid to learners' learning, then they must be an important audience whatever the purpose, mode or technique of assessing.

For assessing to be of maximum value to learners, the learners need to be involved in the assessment process. This must include active involvement in feedback, and may well include involvement with the design and judgement of assessing. The latter are inherent in collaborative assessing discussed on page 110. In distance learning, 'involvement' in feedback may have to be limited to written, or at best telephone, audioconference or computer conferencing with the teacher and other learners. In a face to face situation it can involve more, from simple questions and answers about marked assessment to full negotiation of judgements.

Case studies presented later in this section, and at various parts throughout the book, indicate some of the ways in which communication between learner and teacher about assessments can be organized. It is not the method which is important, but the aims and processes of providing feedback. Many of the approaches more usually associated with evaluating are applicable.

Assessing for teachers

Both formal and informal assessing have applications for the teacher involved in learning. They provide feedback to the teacher about the effectiveness of their teaching (or of their facilitation of learning) as we have previously indicated. In this way the results of assessing may be an aid to course evaluating. In practice it is often a feeling that 'something is wrong with the results' which raises issues and forms the starting point of the spiral of evaluating introduced on page 45. Feedback is also provided which allows the teacher to make informed judgements about the learners, perhaps for purposes of diagnosis and remediation, planning future teaching, report and reference writing, selection or prediction.

Results of assessing, whether they be marks in a mark book, informal impressions or detailed comments arrived at during collaborative assessing are there to be used to help the learners, not just to be kept in a file.

Assessing for 'outsiders'

In the present context, by 'outsiders' we mean those not directly involved in the learning/teaching process being assessed. These may include parents, potential employers, teachers in other organizations and institutions and administrators. In certain circumstances it may include those undertaking educational research or educational psychologists using diagnostic instruments. Although this audience may be less important in the context of assessing for learning, they are often all important to individual learners. An external public examination may well hold the key to college entrance or employment. A profile report may be used by employers to determine job progression. Often, assessing designed with 'outsiders' as the main audience provides very little feedback to either learner or teacher about individual's strengths and weaknesses. A grade C in a public examination does not help the learner plan for future learning (although it may well bar the way for certain learning or employment) nor does it provide much information of use to the teacher to help him or her come to know their own strengths and weaknesses in the learning they have organized. In addition, assessing used in this way as a predictor of some sort may be inappropriate as we have noted previously.

More positively, results of assessing can provide useful information to 'outsiders' if reported with the aim of aiding learning. For example parents are important in helping their children learn. Greater positive contact between institutionalized and everyday educators can help learners learn. Diagnosis of problems, strengths and weaknesses as a result of assessing can be used by parents. It cannot be used unless it is communicated and discussed in a meaningful way. The assessment developments in the National Curriculum in the UK have identified these as important issues.

Communication between different teachers who teach a particular learner, or from one teacher to the next who will be responsible, should be used to provide continuity and facilitate learning. How often do teachers in an institution or organization have meaningful communication about individual learner's strengths, weaknesses and needs, let alone pass on relevant and helpful information to teachers in the learners' future institutions? How often is much time spent 'diagnosing needs' or 'bringing the group up to the required level' when the relevant information could so easily be made available?

How can we assess?

We believe that decisions relating to assessing can make or break a learning situation. We must emphasise that assessing is not only the conventional marking of written work but also includes many other aspects: project or syndicate work, informal feedback (see section 2), self and peer assessing. It is these 'alternatives' which can be focused upon aiding learners learn that we concentrate on in this section and elsewhere in the book.

Learners need not have all their achievements recorded but the learners and the teachers need to see progress throughout the course of learning. Any documentation arising must be that which can be defended to, understood by and accepted by all those involved:

learners, teachers, other organizations and institutions, possible employers. The whole process should be focused on active involvement by the learner in their learning. It is not the actual methods or tools of assessing which we believe should be changed in many cases, rather the underlying philosophy and the aims of their use and application.

There is a vast range of types of assessing available. From informal and casual observations, through teacher organized and marked questions, standardized tests, to assessment criteria devised and used by the learners themselves. All have a place in facilitating learning, but not all may be realistic or desirable in any particular situation. Like all learning/teaching activities, assessing needs to be carefully chosen to suit the intended purposes, expected outcomes and constraints. We do not provide details of specific assessment instruments, but concentrate on highlighting issues which we believe are relevant to the theme of the book: how assessing can be used to facilitate and improve learning. A wide range of instruments can be used, for example comprehension exercises, diagnostic tests, diaries, essay assignments, individual or group discussion, mini research projects, multiple choice, open book tests, oral tests, practical projects, problem solving, profile recording, self assessment questions and questionnaires. It is why and how they are used which are important. Those readers who require details of particular instruments are directed to the bibliography at the end of this section.

When deciding upon assessment techniques, an appropriate starting point is to consider two questions:

- What are the overall purposes, or aims, of assessing?
- Who is the audience for the results of assessing?

These questions have been specifically considered in the previous parts of this section and are recurrent throughout the book. When the aims and audiences of assessing have been discussed and clarified (see the group activities at the end of this section) it is valuable to consider a number of factors or 'modes' relating to assessing before developing the actual technique.

Modes of assessing

Let us consider modes of assessing which we have listed as bipolar constructs:

informal	formal
formative	summative
process	product
criterion referenced	norm referenced
individual focused	group focused
continuous	end point
learner judged	teacher judged
internal	external.

The constructs should not be seen as being absolute or mutually exclusive. For example it is possible to use a particular assessment both formatively **and** summatively, at the same time assessing **both** elements of process and of product. Likewise, the constructs 'continuous -- end-point' and 'course work -- examinations' are in most cases likely to have a close relationship with each other. Nevertheless, consideration of these constructs form a valuable way of discussing factors involved in the choice of an assessment technique or in the analysis of a technique already in use. (The activities at the end of this section give some ideas about discussing the aspects noted above.)

We briefly discuss each of these constructs in turn. Some of the aspects we consider to be more relevant to assessing for learning are subsequently expanded.

Informal – formal

Informal assessing in education, as in all walks of life, is an inevitable and ongoing phenomenon which is often carried out unconsciously. Teachers observe learners, learners observe teachers, both observe learning aids; judgements are made. Formal assessing is more of a planned and often more obtrusive activity. Time is set aside, learners generally realise that they are being assessed, results are said to have a particular purpose which is usually known by both learners and teachers.

Informal assessing plays a very important part in education, often much more difficult to qualify or quantify than that of more formal assessing. Although both teachers and learners are continually assessing events informally, in most institutionalized education the balance of power is towards the teacher. Much information used by teachers is the result of informal assessing: report writing, references, discussion with colleagues, discussion with learners. Negatively, it can be argued that informal assessing is usually subjective, often undertaken covertly and may be the result of personal preferences and dogma. However, it can equally be argued that the majority of informal assessing by teachers is (or at least should be) exercised with the aim of helping learners and teachers become more aware of themselves: their strengths, weaknesses and future needs.

As teachers assess learners informally, the reverse is also constantly happening. Learners' assessments of their teachers have important effects on learning and on the general milieu of the learning environment. Individuals' attitudes towards learning are effected by how the organizers of learning are viewed. Indeed (and unfortunately) learners are sometimes described as jellies who tend to mould and model themselves on their teachers: a motivated teacher leads to a motivated group of learners; a demotivated or lax teacher leads to less than optimum attitudes towards learning. This is as true of adult learners as it is of those in primary schools.

Assessing for learning must involve teachers and learners sharing their informal assessments and judgements, becoming more open and helping each other identify needs, possibilities, strengths and weaknesses. This is a key focus of other sections of the book. Section 2 in particular introduces methods of helping people communicate and share ideas.

Formative – summative

The terms 'formative' and 'summative' which are often used in the context of evaluation, can equally be applied to the intentions of assessing learners. Formative assessing is about using the process and results of assessing to influence (hopefully to facilitate) the learning process. Summative assessing is focused more on using results for some external reason, perhaps for deciding whether or not a particular learner be allowed to continue with a course of study or has achieved the required competencies. It may come at the end of a particular learning experience with which the learner will not be continuing. The distinction is blurred; a terminal test may also help the learner realize their strengths and weaknesses and modify learning (or teaching). However, we wonder if it is reasonable to consider an external public examination as having much of a formative role, other than in preventing certain learners from doing certain things or obtaining certain positions.

To facilitate learning we believe that assessing must have a strong formative role. However this does not prevent the use of summative assessing for certain specific purposes. For formative assessing to have the maximum benefit for learners (and teachers), again it must be carefully planned and undertaken. A mark or short comment on an assignment is unlikely to have much of a formative effect whereas using an assignment (be it written, discursive or practical) to open discussion about learning, about needs, about future learning, has a vast potential.

Process – product

Process and product in learning are closely related: there is unlikely to be any product without process; the product is likely to depend strongly on the process engaged in its production. Most assessment in education and training involves the judgement of some product, be it a loaf baked by learner bakers, an essay assignment, some technological structure or a PhD thesis. Products are easier to assess than processes. A tangible object is easier to judge than the ways in which a group of learners working together interact, come to know each other, become aware of individual strengths, weaknesses and needs; or how an individual explores how to become a self-motivating autonomous learner. Not only is the judgement of products a normal activity within our society, in the context of education it also allows teachers to check and compare their results, an argument being that subjectivity is decreased. In areas of learning where process is considered important, formal assessing is less commonplace: aesthetic or literary appreciation, drama, discussion skills, enterprise skills, learning to cope with new or unusual interpersonal situations, psychomotor skills, to name a few. As in most aspects of assessing, the aims of learning are important: if the aim is to learn to drive a car, then assessing which involves the learner writing an essay about the theory of driving is unlikely to be appropriate.

We consider process assessing to be a very important aspect of learning. It is discussed further on page 105.

Criterion-referenced – norm-referenced

Using the example of assessing for competency discussed earlier, we would more likely be happy if we knew that the pharmacist (or surgeon, or plumber or bus driver etc) had reached a particular level of competence in his or her areas of skill, rather than had obtained slightly in excess of the mean mark in their final assessment before leaving college/training. It would be reassuring to know that the plumber had indeed reached a level of skill such that they were competent at, say, joining two copper pipes using a copper fitting and necessary tools. It is clear that assessments in UK for vocational qualifications and in the National Curriculum have moved firmly in this direction

In these, and many more examples of assessing learning, a score which merely describes the standing of the learner in comparison to his or her peers is of less use to the learners than a score which indicates the level of competence in a number of areas. It is also probably of less use to the teacher and possible employer. The former approach is known as norm-referencing and the latter as criterion-referenced. Stated simply:

- Norm-referenced assessing aims to compare the achievements of the learner with those of other learners.

- Criterion-referenced assessing aims to assess the learner by comparison with some pre-determined or negotiated criteria (eg. a competency or a specified attainment target).

Much has been written about norm and criterion referencing (see the bibliography at the end of this section). Many of the more esoteric articles attempt to define specific delimiters of two distinct ways of assessing, arguing not only that construction, marking and analysis should be different for norm and criterion-referencing, but also that each has its own associated mathematics. Here, we wish only to raise the issue that selection of these particular modes is an important consideration. We believe that it is more the way in which assessing is judged, than the actual instrument used, which indicates criterion or norm referencing. As always, the starting point should be to clarify what the overall purposes of assessing are. If an important purpose is to improve the learning of individual learners then we believe that criterion referencing is the most appropriate mode. It allows both learners and teachers to judge a particular assessment against certain criteria. These criteria may be based on the products or processes of learning and could be unilaterally set by teachers, may be negotiated between learner and teacher, or may be devised by the learner themselves: self-referencing, as applied in self, and possibly peer assessing (see page 110). Whichever method is used, criteria need to be developed (as they do in norm-referenced interpretation) and results need to be judged.

Individual focused – group focused

Assessing focused on the individual aims to describe the individual, help him or her in their learning and help the teacher arrive at a better understanding of the learners' needs. In comparison, group focused assessing aims to provide information about group trends, about overall 'standards', perhaps hoping to present generalized views of large groups so that individual idiosyncrasies and differences are blurred.

The majority of 'public' examinations (College Entrance, those at 16+ and 18+ etc) are group focused as are the various attempts to assess overall standards of a large sample of learners, such as the efforts of the Assessment of Performance Unit in the UK. Even much internal assessing undertaken within schools, colleges and higher education is group focused: scripts are skim read before deciding on the standard for grading; a pre-ordained mark scheme is used based upon group expectations. There is nothing wrong with this approach if it suits the purposes and aims of assessing, but as a method of facilitating learning it falls short. If we wished to assess whether or not a driver who left a public house at closing time is fit to drive, we would observe and assess the individual. It would be little use applying the group statistic that, say, 10% of people leaving public houses at closing time are unfit to drive, therefore every tenth person should be arrested! If assessing is to help learners learn, it must focused on individuals, must take account of individual needs, strengths and weaknesses.

Continuous – end-point

Continuous assessing is generally taken to mean assessing periodically throughout a particular learning process, a procedure which is becoming more commonplace in most areas of institutionalized education. By 'end-point' we mean assessing at the end of a particular learning process, for example a final examination, end of term test or assignment at the end of a course or period of training.

Continuous or periodic assessing may be through course work, examination, oral, written assignment etc. Compared with end point, this type of continuous assessing has certain advantages for learning. For most learners it has the possibility of providing valuable formative feedback about their strengths, weaknesses and needs; it can help reduce stress associated with the contrived 'examination environment'; it can motivate them in to consistent work, and should not unduly penalize for one or two below par pieces of assessed work. However for such advantages to be realized in practice, the organization of continuous assessing needs to be focused on the needs of the learners. It is insufficient merely to set several essays rather than one, only providing a raw grade or mark as feedback. Likewise, several in-course examinations where only an overall mark is provided is likely to do no more for learning than an end-point examination. Accumulation of credits for competencies and attainments may also provide problems unless there is appropriate formative feedback with discussion and analysis. The focus should be the improvement of the quality and process of learning. As always the approach and process of assessing is all important. Where much emphasis is placed on marks, on grades, on comparison and certification some of the potential benefits to learning will be lost. Where only some assignments are identified as 'counting towards an overall grade' others are likely to receive less attention from learners. The balance and the negotiations with learners are crucial.

When discussing informal internal modes of assessing, 'continuous assessing' can take on a new meaning:

- not only assessing at intervals, but also taking active account of the continual and natural processes of informal assessing

- using results to open discussion, share ideas and aid learning.

Assessing need then not be something 'done to' learners, but 'done with' learners, indeed sometimes 'done by' learners too.

Learner judged – teacher judged

In everyday life we are constantly judging events that directly involve ourselves or our peers. Whilst the learner car driver is judged by their teacher, and later by an examiner (teacher-assessed), they also make their own critical judgements of their actions and abilities (self-assessed). When the test is finally passed, friends will be all too willing to pass judgement on the new driver's abilities (peer-assessed)!

In institutionalized education and training, the majority of learner assessment is unilaterally undertaken by the 'teacher' who may be the person directly involved in 'teaching' the learners or who may be external to the process (for example an examiner in a public examination). Rarely are learners given the responsibility and freedom to assess and judge their own learning. Responsibility could be vested in individual learners, in groups of learners working together or in a collaborative process involving both learners and teachers. Self, peer and collaborative assessing have an important role to play in the shifting of emphasis from teaching to learning. We consider these modes of assessing later in this section.

Internal – external

Internal assessing involves those actually participating in the learning/ teaching process having control over the assessment. Learners, teachers who are involved with the learners, and others closely involved in the learning process (perhaps parents, youth leaders, laboratory technicians) are all sources of internal assessing. External assessing on the other hand involves an 'outsider' someone brought-in for the purpose of assessing. Such include examiners in public examinations, driving test examiners, educational psychologists etc.

Where emphasis is upon informal, formative, process, individual focused or learner-judged modes of assessing, it is most probable that 'insiders' will be involved. Other modes may well involve internal or external assessing. For example a formal, largely summative, assessment may be carried out by the learner's teacher, by an external teacher, or by a combination. The latter is common in higher education in the UK where an external examiner is appointed to moderate internally set and marked assessments. These assessments may be end-point (as in a degree examination) or may be continually set assignments. The role and power of the external examiner is variable, generally acting as adviser and arbiter rather than final judge.

While internal assessing is accepted in higher education and adult training and education, at other levels misgivings are often expressed. These are particularly strong in the case of end-point or summative assessing, where the main purposes are to classify and certificate. Here the argument is often used that external assessing allows comparison with other learners and therefore provides the ability to monitor overall standards, both local and national. Moves towards this mode of assessing can easily be seen in many countries. For example in the UK the Assessment of Performance Unit has been set-up by the Government to assess and monitor standards reached by school learners. It is clear that the assessments associated with the UK National Curriculum have a similar role. In some states progression of learners between grades depends on adequate performance; in most states in the USA, units have been set up to monitor basic skills in the schools. Earlier liberal and learner-centred assessment systems in Denmark are giving way to systems which emphasise external standards in formal assessment.

Emphasis on external assessing does little to promote the type of learning we suggest throughout this book. However, internal assessing has an important role to play in helping learners learn, in helping teachers know the needs of learners in helping others (eg employers) come to know what it is a particular individual can do. The frameworks associated with credit, competency or attainment accumulation have important expectations for internal as well as external assessment.

We believe that certain modes are particularly appropriate to 'assessing for learning', in particular those which tend towards:

- criterion-referenced

- formative

- process

- individually focused

- internal.

Aspects relating to these modes are now discussed in greater depth.

Assessing process

In most areas of life, processes as well as products are all important. Likewise in much institutionalized education and training, process is a very important aspect, particularly when learning involves interacting, or when the learner is engaging in the role of generator or receiver described in section 4. Assessing these processes can facilitate learning. Also, as we noted in section 1, different learners have different preferred ways of learning, their preferred processes of learning are different. Assessing these processes can help the teacher and other learners come to know each other, to better understand each others need, to minimize any mismatch between teaching and learning.

> Starting from a product (a loaf of bread baked by learner bakers) the learners and teachers involved discuss and assess the processes that went to make each loaf. For example shape, size, finish are related to what was actually done during each part of making and baking. Learners are actively involved in constructive criticism and see it as a natural part of their learning process. Assessing in this way helps learners learn from

each other's work and helps the teacher become sensitive to needs and problems.

Much informal assessing is of processes. The teacher writing a reference or report on a learner is likely to have formed opinions by watching process: how the learner interacts with others, their attitude towards learning, the contributions made to group work etc. The driving instructor watches what the learner driver does, modifying their instruction in the light of these processes. The learners in informally assessing their teacher are likely to focus on processes: how the teacher teaches, rather than on product: what is learned.

However, most formal assessing of learners undertaken within institutionalized education is of products: the written assignment, a drawing or sculpture, the laboratory notebook. Even in those parts of learning where much emphasis is placed on what we describe elsewhere as 'loving' aspects (interpersonal, development of group dynamics, learning to help one another learn, working together) if assessment is undertaken it is often of a written, reflective nature. This is not surprising, teachers are used to product assessment, it is easier to manage, more tangible and convenient, easier to moderate than assessing process. Assessing process is more overtly subjective than that of the majority of products: it occurs in real time, there is little or no chance of 'going back to check' or of 'taking it home' to assess. In much of real life (as opposed to institutionalized education and training) process is inferred from product: car crashes are reconstructed from their products, skid marks, positioning of vehicles, damage caused. Scientists often infer process from the effects and the products of some change or interaction.

Many investigations into 'how teachers teach' concentrate on process. From observations of student teachers to detailed and complex observation and interaction analysis, the focus is on process rather than product. For example the observation schedule outlined on page 61 concentrates on various teacher/learner interactions. The outcome here may well be products: written descriptions of process, or video or audio recordings of the teaching learning process which go some way towards providing a record for discussion and analysis after the event.

Within a more usual learner/teacher situation there are approaches to assessing, both formal and informal, which can facilitate development of process.

A major assignment for a module in audio-visual communications involves the learners in a group television production. Learners work in groups of 6-8 to develop a short recording of a topic of their own choice. The product is seen as less important than the processes involved. At the start of the assignment the teacher stresses that a major aim is to develop group interaction and cooperation, indicating that team work is necessary for a satisfactory production. Reasons for this approach are indicated and discussed.

During production, much emphasis is placed on discussion and negotiation, both between the group members and between learners and teacher. Other groups of learners are engaged upon different work (eg. graphics), but often act as consultants and observers to the group involved in production. Much work is undertaken outside timetabled sessions and learners are asked to keep individual diaries of what they do, how much time is spent, what problems arose and how these were overcome. During timetabled sessions, diaries are discussed between the learners and teachers, focus being upon what was done, how it was done and how this relates to the activities of other group members.

During practical TV work, many of the learners not directly involved, together with the teacher and technicians, observe, help and suggest alternative approaches. Emphasis is on facilitating group processes and encouraging learning, rather than upon an expert 'showing how it should be done'.

At the end of each session a discussion is held where learners are encouraged to reflect critically on the processes engaged in. Assessing is based on the observation of process, diaries of events and group discussions together with the product. It is negotiated between learners, technicians and teacher.

Assessing used in this way is of an essentially formative nature with focus upon involvement of the learners in the assessment process. It is obviously internal, involves both learner and teacher judgement and is a continuous process. The key to the assessing is communication between learners, between learners and teachers and others involved. In the above case study an overall summative grade (demanded by the course validation) is also given based to a large extent upon the processes previously assessed and discussed.

The techniques of assessing process noted in the case study draw heavily upon those more usually associated with evaluating (see section 2). Indeed, other techniques such as observation schedules, snowballing and brainstorming lend themselves to formative process assessing, as do role play and simulation (for example an in-tray exercise where learners are presented with information about a particular issue or subject and asked to work either together or alone to reach conclusions or a decision). These techniques lay stress on the formative nature of assessing.

Formative assessing

As we have previously indicated, a formative mode of assessing aims to use the process of assessing to facilitate learning. This, we believe, must be a major aim of assessing for learning. Whether assessing is primarily criterion- or norm-referenced, informal or formal, process or product, to have a formative role there must be meaningful communication between assessed and assessor. To be really formative we believe that assessing must involve discussion between those involved; groups of learners or learners and teachers. Such discussion may arise during a number of activities: informal questioning during learning/teaching, groups of learners working together on a project or syndicate work, specific feedback from the teacher (or peers) about an assessed piece of work. If discussion can involve setting-up the assessment aims and criteria, so much the better.

> To help provide formative feedback to learners about their written assignments, the pro-forma shown in figure 3.2 is completed by the assessor. This may be either the teacher or one or more peers depending upon the particular assignment.
>
> These written comments are used as the basis of subsequent discussion between those involved. Generally this discussion is undertaken individually between assessed and assessor(s). In the case of peers being the assessors, they may or may not invite the teacher to be present (in practice, they usually do!). If any issues of a general nature arise from these discussions, time is set aside for discussion with the complete group.
>
> Although it may appear that this approach takes too much time, in practice this is not the case. Much learning is by learners working on assignments on their own or in groups rather than in more formal classes taken by the teacher.

The above case study indicates one possible method of providing feedback to learners. There are many others. For example comprehensive 'notes in the margin' or at the end of an assignment; verbal (or non-verbal) feedback during discussion in class; computer marked multiple-choice items, all provide feedback to the learner. Self-assessment questions embedded in learning material, or at the end of a section, can usefully cause the learner to reflect and self assess.

ASSIGNMENT ATTACHMENT

Student's name:

Assignment Title.   Unit No.

NOTES

Sections left blank are not relevant to this assignment.

Some aspects are more important than others, so there is no formula connecting the number of ticks in different boxes with the grade.

A tick in the left-hand box means that the statement on the left is true: a tick in the second box from the left means that the statement on the left is true to some extent. Similarly for the right-hand boxes. eg.

Topic covered in depth ☐ ☐ ☑ ☐ Superficial treatment of topic
means that the topic was treated somewhat superficially in the assignment.

Ticks in the right-hand boxes show areas of deficiency in the report.

Itemized Rating Scale

STRUCTURE
← →

| All goals covered | Little relationship to goals |
| Topic covered in depth | Superficial treatment of topic |

ARGUMENT

Accurate presentation of evidence	Much evidence inaccurate or questionable
Logically developed argument	Essay rambles and lacks continuity
Original and creative thought	Little evidence of originality
Relevant use of own experience	Little evidence of own experience

SOURCES

| Adequate acknowledgement of sources | Inadequate acknowledgement of sources |
| Correct citation of references | Incorrect referencing |

STYLE

| Fluent piece of writing | Clumsily written |
| Succinct writing | Unnecessarily repetitive |

PRESENTATION

| Legible & well set out work | Untidy and difficult to read |
| Reasonable length | Over/under length |

MECHANICS

| Effective use of figures & tables | Figures & tables add little to argument |

EXPLANATION AND COMMENTS:

```
┌──────────────────────────────┐
│ GRADE:                       │
│                              │
│                              │
└──────────────────────────────┘
```

TUTOR: . . . .   DATE: . . . .

Figure 3.2 *Pro forma for formative feedback*

It may not always be possible to achieve the contact and two way communication we believe to be so valuable. In distance learning written comments from tutor to learner may be all that is generally possible. At times these could be supported by telephone audioconference or computer conferencing, but this may not always be convenient. It is not the method but the quality and intent of feedback which is all important in helping learners learn. Feedback can have very negative effect on learners as all teachers (and learners) know too well!

Collaborative, peer and self-assessing

Traditionally, most formal institutionalized educational assessing is controlled unilaterally by teachers who set the criteria, mark the learner's products and provide varying degrees of feedback to the learner and/or others. At the opposite end of the spectrum is the learner who, say undertaking a practical project or written work, sets their own goals, continually monitors their work against personally set criteria and judges the final outcome. These two 'models' represent extremes of a continuum indicating the degree of autonomy vested in the learner for his or her learning, as indicated in figure 3.3.

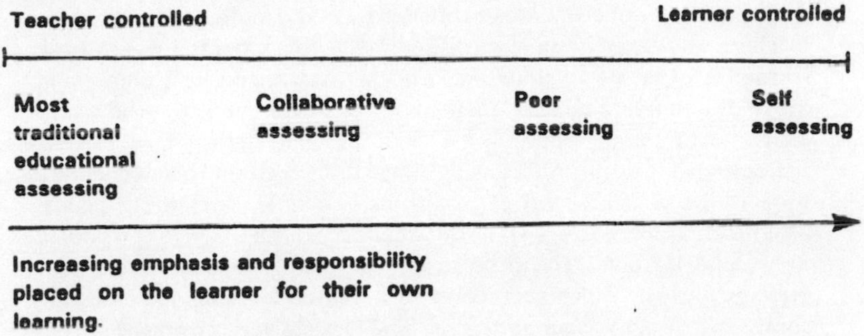

Teacher controlled   **Learner controlled**

| Most traditional educational assessing | Collaborative assessing | Peer assessing | Self assessing |

Increasing emphasis and responsibility placed on the learner for their own learning.

Figure 3.3 *Degrees of learner autonomy in assessing*

In education, little account is generally taken of the right hand side of this continuum although it is continually incorporated in learning, for example the person designing and building a construction in wood, developing their performance for a dramatic production, or writing an assignment. Here we focus upon this side of the continuum.

Collaborative assessing involves discussion and negotiation between learner and teacher about assessment criteria, methods and any grading. Peer assessing either involves discussion and negotiation between the learners and their peers, or may be assessment undertaken by one or more peers apart from the individual learner being assessed. By self-assessing we mean a self-directed and determining learner setting their own assessment criteria, judging their learning processes (or products) against these criteria, and making decisions based on these judgements. The learner may well also have set their own goals for learning, determined their own programme of study and performed the learning deemed necessary. This is obviously very different from the majority of assessing currently in use in education and training.

We see collaborative assessing as being the most immediately applicable move towards greater involvement of learners in the processes of assessing and facilitating learning. It is probably also more acceptable than the use of self- or peer-assessing to the majority of learners and teachers used to the unilateral autonomy of teachers. In collaborative assessing, the teacher and learner (and possibly also peers) are actively involved in the assessment process. There are a variety of ways this can be achieved in practice, from negotiating and agreeing all aspects of learning leading to a particular assessment, to negotiating final marks on a more traditionally teacher set assessment.

A major aspect of the assessment of an in-service diploma course for teachers and trainers involves 'integrative assignments', where each learner is expected to draw on concepts developed in a number of modules and relate these to their own work experience to produce an assignment for assessment.

Learners are drawn from a wide range of backgrounds, and display a wide range of needs and expectations. To help meet these needs, assignment titles, content and assessment is negotiated between course tutors and learners. The process is a multistage one involving progressive focusing which culminates in a written learning and assessing contract between learner and tutor. The process varies over the period of the course; as time progresses greater autonomy is vested in the individual learners. (Here, we focus on the aspects of assessing, further details of this study are given on page 157).

Each module has one or more assignments associated with it, these may be written or may use audiovisual media. Completion dates and guideline starting dates for a term's assignments are negotiated with the complete group. These take into account completion of relevant modules and aim to minimize 'bunching' of work load.

Prior to the starting date of a particular assignment, learners are asked to consider what it is they wish to do and to prepare personal notes outlining their aims, likely content and format of assignments. These notes include the assessment criteria the learner would like to use for assessment of their work.

Close to the agreed starting date, time is set aside for each member of the group to briefly outline their proposed assignment (including assessment criteria) to peers and tutor. The process is formative and highly supportive to individuals, who generally modify their outlines in the light of these discussions.

Individual learners and the tutor meet to negotiate a 'contract' which specifies details of the assignment and assessment. Details of assessment generally include:

- who will assess (peers and/or collaboration between learner and tutor)

- criteria for assessing (eg. against assignment objectives, impression, process, product)

- distribution of assessment grades.

Although agreed at this juncture, learners are free to renegotiate during the process of their assignment.

The assignment is handed in (generally on time: agreement and negotiation of dates places a responsibility on the learner not usually apparent in more unilaterally set work) and is assessed. Where collaborative assessing is the chosen mode, learner and teacher meet to discuss the assignment and together negotiate around the previously agreed criteria. Where peer assessing has been chosen, negotiation is either amongst the chosen peers, or between peers and learner.

It must be noted that the process outlined above is developed over a period of time, particularly where peer assessing is involved. Learners need much help and encouragement initially, but generally react very favourably as they become more familiar with the technique. The process has a very marked positive effect on the relationships between learners and teachers.

In the above case study, both the topic of the assignment and the assessment criteria are subject to negotiation. It is equally possible, although we believe less effective, to use collaborative (or even peer) assessing for judging assessments which have been set by the teacher. This may form a useful intermediate stage for many teachers and learners, and could be applied to, for example, essay questions, problem solving exercises and many forms of practical work. In the case study it is product which is being assessed; similar techniques could well be used for process. The approach is equally applicable to course work or end-point assessing, and is individually focused and formative.

We see peer- and self-assessing in education as being very closely related, particularly where one is learning alongside other learners: self-assessing takes place in relation to the activities of peers, their goals, criteria, judgements, processes and products. Judgements made during self-assessing are modified by feedback from peers. This is likely to be so to a lesser or greater extent in most distance learning. Very little organized learning takes place in complete isolation from peers.

Part of a training course for teachers involves personal presentations where each group member gives a 10-15 minute presentation of their own choice to a small group of their peers. Presentations are video recorded by one of the group. A major aim is to encourage group discussion about teaching styles. At the end of each presentation, the group replay recordings and discuss the presentation. Enabling and constraining factors are analysed and evaluated.

In practice, groups are very supportive whilst at the same time generating much constructive criticism of use to both the presenter and other group members. Generally, learners indicate that they find the experience both useful and enjoyable. The group dynamic is certainly improved.

The use of self- and peer-assessing in a formal context may pose a large challenge to teachers, and learners, more used to a unilateral control and decision making process in educational assessing. Nevertheless, we believe that both self- and peer-assessing are important in the context of learners taking greater responsibility for their learning.

It will be clear from the preceding pages that we have purposely expressed a particular view about the modes of assessing most likely to promote the learner's responsibility for learning. Often these are at variance with the dominant modes found within most institutionalized education and training. We make no apology for this. In a move from teaching to learning, from learners receiving to becoming actively involved, from teachers performing to becoming conductors and facilitators of learning, there is need for a change in emphasis of assessing. The change must be supported by training, discussion and critical analysis amongst all those involved, teachers, learners, employers, parents. Finally, it must be remembered that assessing learners, whatever mode or method is used, can and should be used to provide valuable feedback to both the learner and the teacher about their needs and about their own successes and failures.

Criteria for assessing

The processes of judging an assessment are carried out against certain criteria. This is so whether the judging is the sole province of the teacher, a collaborative venture between teacher and learner, or undertaken by peers or the learner themselves. These criteria can be arrived at in a number of ways, via: objectives, contracts between learner and teacher and impressions.

The vast majority of learning and teaching is undertaken with particular objectives, competencies or attainments in mind, although perhaps not the formally written pre-specified detailed objectives often discussed in educational texts. Criteria for assessing should be related to the objectives of learning. To take an extreme example, if the objective of a particular part of learning was to be able to recall four sources of assessment criteria, then assessing the learner's

knowledge of the brainstormimg technique would be a most inappropriate way of either facilitating or assessing the particular learning.
This is obviously exaggerated, but how often is assessing poorly related
to the objectives of learning? How often is a particular level of
learning, for example problem solving and transfer of knowledge,
assessed by methods which require staightforward recall of knowledge? Not only is the assessment an inappropriate way of monitoring
the learning, but worse it is likely to have a detrimental effect on the
learner's motivation to learn.

Where objectives for particular learning are specified and are known
by both learners and teacher, these form a useful basis for developing
assessment criteria. The idea is appropriate to all the modes of
assessing we have previously identified. It is equally applicable to
affective, cognitive, psychomotor and interpersonal learning, whether
the learning experience is wholly negotiated between learner and
teacher, an individual is working as an autonomous self-directing
learner, or learning is controlled by the teacher.

The source of objectives against which to assess is ultimately the
views, feelings and beliefs of those involved: the teachers, 'outside'
teachers (for example examination boards, external examiners, mod-
erators) often outsiders (eg employers, governors) and hopefully the
learners. These beliefs are a complex product of the education or
training system and the society within which the individuals operate.

Criteria arrived at through negotiation and discussion between
learners and teachers can result in an assessment 'contract' as we have
discussed in detail on Page 000. Criteria derived in this way are fully
known and should be acceptable to both parties. The learner is
involved in the assessment procedures from the outset, and therefore
the criteria which are to be used for judgement should have a good
relationship to the learning which takes place. Any apparent mismatch
could well form the basis of renegotiation of the 'contract'. The case
study on page 112 describes one particular application of contract type
assessing.

Impression (or romantic) assessing involves the assessor reading,
looking at or discussing the aspect being assessed and deriving their
comment or grade depending upon the impressions made. To a
varying extent, most assessing has a degree of this approach however
objective one considers they are being. Problems exist where the
teacher is assessing unilaterally: the learner has no or little knowledge
of criteria being used and therefore may be unable to respond in a

meaningful way. Criteria and interpretation may well change from one assessment to another, again causing difficulties for the learners.

However, impression assessing can form a very good basis from which learner and teacher can discuss the assessment. Ideas and feelings of both learner and teacher can be explored, and the reasons for impressions and interpretations can be explored.

Suggested group activities

1. Why does assessing take such a key position in much education and training?

Use a snowball or brainstorm technique (see section 2). If possible try to include learners in the group discussing the question.

2. Who is a particular assessment intended for?

We have found that analysis of a case study is a valuable starting point. For example, one or more of the group could be asked to bring to a meeting brief case study examples of who uses the results of a particular assessment. The whole group may discuss and analyse the case study, or alternatively sub-groups could report back after analysis.

3. What modes of assessment should be used?

A structured discussion using pages 97–105 of this section as a resource could be organized.

4. How do you (or your department/institution):
● add together marks from various assessments
● analyse the marks given in one or more assessments
● feedback results of assessment to learners?

If you are working in a group all the better, particularly if the group includes some learners. Possible ways of facilitating group work for these activities are to use either snowballing or brainstorming (see section 2).

5. How can learner's attitudes towards a particular approach to learning be assessed?

The group could be asked to either read an example case study (eg the one given on page 112) of a learning situation, or better focus on an example taken from one of the group members. Use either brainstorming or snowballing (see section 2) to generate ideas which can then be discussed and evaluated.

6. Design assessment procedures for a particular group of learners which will involve the learners discussing between themselves their own learning problems

The group considering this could be divided into smaller groups of, say four-six people. Each could be asked to consider the same issue but using a different technique. For example one group may be given a case study example to discuss and transfer to their own area. Another could brainstorm or snowball, another could use the services of an 'expert' input. All groups should report back at the end.

Difficulties and criticisms

Assessing is currently viewed as being primarily for giving information to other educational establishments, employers or teachers on a succeeding course. The bases of these assessment are an explicit or implicit normal distribution (eg. 20% of learners at 16 pass this examination, implying that it is passed by the top 20% of the ability range and that a grade A or grade 1 will probably be about the top 4-5%). Whilst the examination may not have been designed with this in mind, it will probably be marked or moderated this way.

Even when teachers mark work handed back to learners that is not used as part of the certification process outlined above, there is a tendency to give marks or grades on this basis. The comments made on a piece of work may be brief, encouraging or discouraging, but the learner has little idea of the basis of the mark which is why we used an example of a feedback form to give the learner some reasons for the grade or mark.

The way that we have suggested using assessments is alien to current practice, the implementation may take more time and energy than current practice. The initial gains would be obvious. The change in relationship between learner and teacher would be considerable. The teacher's role would change from an expert pontificating to a mentor assisting. The change is also from a subject expert to a problem solver and facilitator of learning. Most training courses for teachers do not focus on problem solving, the courses are run on a conventional didactic approach often associated with the 'sitting with Nellie' approach. Is a 50% load on teaching practice the right way to train a teacher or should the training include a smaller load and much more on problem solving strategies? Obviously we are open to criticism for using a book as a means of trying to get learners into a problem solving mode, although we hope that our recent students would recognise our own attempts to move away from a didactic approach.

We may have implied that current practices are wrong, whereas our own intention is to identify alternative practice focused on helping the learner to learn rather than comparing and reporting to others. We have also tried to show that alternative approaches enable more useful reporting. However that change also implies that employers and others who use the results of assessing have to learn a new means of communication. With the plethora of recent assessment methods (graded tests, criterion-referenced tests, competency tests, profiles, personal records) employers are already raising their arms in horror and asking for a return to the previous diplomas and certificates which they 'understood'. The chances of moving a stage further is obviously loaded with difficulties. Are education and training about providing reports to outsiders or enabling the learners to learn? Are these necessarily incompatible?

A further inertia that the teachers experience is with competitive comparative assessing. Teachers are usually the ones who succeeded in the previous system so there is a certain pride in a system in which you succeeded. Is it a minority who are dissatisfied and are raising questions in the way that we have done? Why are national, state, county and local authorities moving away from the current comparative system? Has the system become so discredited with the general public that it is politically worthwhile to change? How does one persuade teachers who are often alienated by government decisions to see the pragmatic and political merit of change? Would there be improved communication with learners, parents and employers? How can the changed system be explained to those audiences? The explanation involves yet more work, the changed assessment system involves yet more work, where is the time coming from in a falling rolls, reduced finance environment? Won't the effort be at the expense of helping learners?

The assumption behind many of the assessment proposals we have suggested is that the learners are willing and able to take on responsibility for their own learning and assessing. The evidence from current practice would suggest that the assumption is untenable especially when associated with a steady increase in unemployment leading to further alienation from those in deprived urban areas. We can only provide the limited evidence available from mastery learning, tutor-based learning, resource-based learning, supported self-study, distance study, open learning and some management training. Agreed that the motivation is high, but does the motivation lead or follow the methods? All these methods depend heavily on feeding back information to learners, assisting them in learning and giving them responsibility for their own learning and assessing.

Annotated bibliography

Anderson, P H and Lawton, L (1992)
A Survey of Methods Used for Evaluating Student Performance on Business Simulations
Simulations and Gaming, 23, 4, 490-98.
Applies Bloom's taxonomy to analyse a range of assessment methods used by teachers to assess learner performance on business simulations.

Ashworth, A E (1982)
Testing for Continuous Assessment
London: Evans.
Although the title indicates emphasis on continuous assessment, the text has wider applicability, examining briefly the reasons for testing, test design and construction, marking and statistical analysis.

Assiter, A and Fenwick, A (1992)
Profiling in Higher Education

London: CNAA.
The report outlines reasons for profiling and considers the types of profiling systems, how they may be developed, how to determine learning outcomes on which the systems are based and more general issues related to assessment.

Black, H D and Dockerell, W B (1980)
Diagnostic Assessment in Secondary Schools
Edinburgh: Scottish Council for Research in Education.
This short book discusses the meaning and applications of diagnostic assessment. Techniques for the construction of diagnostic tests are demonstrated, including the problems involved. The implications for teachers and pupils actually using diagnostic assessment are considered.

Bloom, B S, Madaus, G F, and Hastings, J T (1981)
Evaluation to Improve Learning
New York: McGraw Hill.
The book is about assessing students' learning. It is aimed at classroom teachers, with a focus on the improvement of students learning. There are sections covering issues such as: objectives; learning for mastery; summative, diagnostic and formative assessment; writing and selecting items for various levels of cognitive learning.

Boud, D (ed) (1988)
Developing Student Autonomy in Learning
London: Kogan Page.
Practicing teachers from around the world working in higher education describe their personal experiences of introducing alternatives to the traditional mode of teaching, course design and assessing. The issues of student, peer and teacher assessment are discussed. Case studies are given about the ways professional teachers have confronted the issues in areas such as independent study, self-directed learning and contract learning.

Boud, D (1992)
The Use of Self-assessment Schedules in Negotiated Learning
Studies in Higher Education,17, 2, 137-49.
Describes an approach to assessment where students create a comprehensive and analytical summary of their learning. This self-

assessment schedule helps capture and account for a wide range of formal and informal learning.

Brewer, I M (1985)
Learning More and Teaching Less: A Decade of Innovation in Self-instruction and Small Group Learning.
Guildford: SRHE and NFER Nelson.
Describes an attempt by the author over a long period to examine and improve ways of promoting learning in higher education. The move from traditional teaching to a mixture of small group work, problem-solving discussion and peer group interaction is described in detail. Assessment involves a wide range of techniques aimed at assessing learner's higher order skills in addition to the more normal recall.

Broadfoot, P M (1979)
Communication in the Classroom: A Study of the Role of Assessment in Motivation
Educational Review, 31, 1, 3-10.
The paper examines the motivation of pupils, particularly the less able. The alienating effect of the assessment process is investigated. Assessment is used as a one sided process rather than an interactive process. A view is put forward that continuous exchange of perceptions and evaluations should enhance motivation by (a) improving the status and self-esteem of the pupil (b) encouraging positive thinking by the pupils about their progress (c) understanding the teachers aims better. Some findings are given from a study involving pupils in their own assessments.

Broadfoot, P (1979)
Assessment, Schools and Society
London: Methuen.
Examines the need for, and roles of, assessment within the context of schools (and other institutions) as a part of society. Assessment and examinations are studied as instruments of social control and their effects upon everyday classroom life is explored. The origins of formal assessment together with newer developments in accountability, performance assessment and informal techniques are dealt with.

Burgess, T and Adams, E (eds) (1980)
Outcomes of Education

London: Macmillan.
Describes various systems of profile recording in schools and higher education. Outlines many of the problems and possibilities of profile recording. Contains many references.

Di Carlo, A and Trentin, G (1990)
Diagnostic Testing in Formative Assessment: the Students as Test Developers
In Bell, C D (ed) *World Yearbook of Education: 1990. Assessment and Evaluation.*
London: Kogan Page.
By acting as authors, students are more responsible as to what they learn and how they learn it. This leads them to test their knowledge through critical revision. The experiment described shows how students developed a computer-based test from an analysis of a hierarchical model of content. The tests were used by the developers and their peers.

Ericson, D P (1984)
Of Minima and Maxima: the Social Significance of Minimal Competency Testing and the Search for Educational Excellence
American Journal of Education, 92, 3, 245-261.
The paper provides a critical review of the use of mastery type tests based on criteria within the high school diploma. It identifies the problem that when large proportions achieve mastery the diploma is devalued. Who decides the arbitrary cut off of mastery and non-mastery, how can it be justified? The idea of such assessments being diagnostic and remedial conflicts with the use of the diploma to select those who are to progress to the next system or grade level.

Good, H (1978)
Interview Marking of Examination Scripts
Assessment and Evaluation in Higher Education, 3, 2, 122-138.
The paper describes a system of marking examination scripts in discussion with students. The argument is based on teacher accountability for the time spent in assessing students and a survey of staff and students who were involved in the process. It also enables feedback to students on end point certification type of assessment.

Harris, N D C (1975)
What is Assessment?

Assessment in Higher Education, 1, 1, 5-12.
A brief outline of a variety of ways of viewing assessment: predictive, diagnostic, comparative, absolute, formative and summative.

Miller, C and Parlett, M (1974)
Up to the Mark: A Study of the Examination Game
Guildford: SRHE.
A study of examinations, their use, and students reactions to a variety of methods used at Edinburgh University. The authors identify two groups of students: cue-seeker and cue-deaf students. In an environment where teachers are also examiners, the former group appear to be at an advantage.

Murphy, R and Torrance, J (1988)
The Changing Face of Educational Assessment
Milton Keynes: Open University Press.
This book is grounded in a broad programme of research into educational assessment which sought to document and analyse new approaches, playing particular regard to their curicula and pedagogic implications. The social and political aspects of assessment are considered.

Nixon, N J (1990)
Assessment Issues in Relation to Experience-based Learning Within Courses
In Bell, C D (ed) *World Yearbook of Education: 1990. Assessment and Evaluation.*
London: Kogan Page.
The main focus is on the assessment of undergraduate sandwich courses, specifically with reference to two issues: what are the aspects of supervised work-experience that should be assessed, and what are the most appropriate forms of assessment available. Examples of assessment systems are provided.

Open University (1981)
Measuring Learning Outcomes (E364 Block 4 Education Studies)
Milton Keynes: Open University Press.
Identifies the different purposes of measuring learning outcomes and the extent to which these purposes dictate the methods employed. The strengths and weaknesses of methods are considered and these are

related to uses in the classroom. Ideas are given for designing tests, examinations and observation schedules.

Rowntree, D (1987)
Assessing Students: How Shall We Know Them?
London: Kogan Page.
A comprehensive and original analysis of the reasons for, methods and effects of assessing learners. Rowntree is constructively critical of much current assessment used in education and suggests that the purposes be reexamined with greater focus on learning.

Rowntree, D (1981)
Statistics Without Tears
London: Harper and Row.
A clear straightforward introduction to the range, scope and utility of statistics in education. The book does not concentrate on how to calculate, rather on the underlying concepts and interpretation of statistics.

Section 4. Roles of learners and teachers

Section 4. Roles of learners and teachers

Section 4. Roles of learners and teachers

Introduction

In the types of learning environment that we are advocating, learning is seen as a shared experience focused around the learner. In this section we are developing an idea of the roles that learners have in various types of learning. We shall refer to the four types of learning activity elaborated in section 1 (ie. memorising, decoding, creating, loving).

These cover a spectrum from the taxi driver memorising streets, through the study of technical subjects with their own specialist language (jargon), problem solving, creating new solutions and ideas to the development of interpersonal relationships. Obviously each of these types of learning has implications for learning environments and the role of teachers.

Rather than consider a one-to-one relationship between teaching and learning we are using a series of metaphors to describe the roles of teachers: composer, conductor, performer, critic. This musical analogy is elaborated further, although the expectations are implied with a mixture of systematic planning, individual differences, coordination, aesthetic and artistic ability as well as skills and criticisms. We discuss the roles of teachers and learners related to assessing and evaluating procedures and the changing responsibility of the learner.

Roles of learners

The learning activities that learners carry out (ie. memorising, decoding, creating, loving) are considered in the context of four possible learner roles: receiver, detective, generator, and facilitator.

At first sight there may appear to be a simple relationship between receiver and memorising and between facilitator and loving. It is our contention that the relationships between learning activities and learner roles is not that simple. Additionally, preferred learning styles of learners interact to make a description of the learning process even more complex (see page 16).

Receiver role

Let us consider the learner sitting in a lecture theatre or classroom being showered with words, pictures, diagrams, lectures, books, experiments, computer programs, face to face conversations and television. There is an over abundance of signals and stimuli to receive. The human brain filters out many of these signals. The learner has to create decoding strategies based on their own experience in order to cope with the filtering and rearranging of this wide range of data, information and experience. This filtering and re-arranging enables the learner to make sense of the vast array of information and to place it in their own context based on their previous experiences from both within and outside institutionalized learning.

The receiver role may involve all of the learning activities. For example, from experience of previous learning, some learners may use a variety of note-taking strategies from headings and subheadings to mind maps, from mnemonics to picture association. Each is using strategies in a creative way to decode material to be memorised into a format which the learner feels helps them to remember. Unfortunately, learners often assume that a learning environment aimed at decoding is in fact aimed at memorising. Learners may then use their energies and apparent role to focus on the wrong types of activity.

As we have noted above, the learner as receiver has a large amount of decoding to undertake. Here, decoding enables stimuli from print, experience or oral contacts to fit into existing life experiences and enables the learner to recode information back into an acceptable form, often via memorising. The use of mnemonic and other memorising strategies is a form of decoding. This decoding may involve creating new associations and interactions to aid memorising.

The loving activity of learning is not out of place with the receiver role. Many learners find that involvement in syndicates with other learners can enhance their learning. In all aspects of memorising from cognitive to psychomotor, from affective to interpersonal the assistance, support and criticism of a peer is often necessary.

Detective role

The detective is a different role where the learner again has a whole array of stimuli. However the assumption behind the use of these stimuli is different: that of discovery. This discovery may not be new to experts, but may be new to the learner. Here, memorising is used to identify strategies that were successful on previous occasions in searching, analysing and communicating. The decoding activity is obviously crucial in this role. Analysis may create 'new' information or result in the creation of alternative types of communication. Finding out the responses of others (a loving activity) is also an important aspect in eliciting responses and assisting peers.

Generator role

The generator is the role where new ideas, new communications (eg artistic) and new ways of viewing events are created. Again, memorising and decoding are important aspects. The memorising is more subliminal, involving passive recourse to memory rather than actively recalling. Strategies, environments and experiences which enhance the role may be memorised and recalled actively, but conventional cognitive and psychomotor skills are probably not used so actively in this role. Decoding is crucial but is more likely in the sense of decoding one's own thoughts, ideas and presentations. Creating is obviously related to the generator role, although that creating may be a long hard labour for some, and a more spontaneous activity for others. The loving aspect is more doubtful in this role. Some people as generators need solitude and isolation (eg some artists and writers) while others find social contact more essential.

Facilitator role

The facilitator role focuses on interpersonal relationships and helping others to learn. 'Others' may be fellow learners, colleagues or even teachers. Again, each of the four learning activities is involved. Memorising is more about remembering names, individual sensitivities, likes and dislikes. Decoding is about watching for and feeling for tensions, visual and facial signals, listening for oral signals, feeling body space and territory. Creating involves using those decoded signals and providing personal signals which enable, inhibit, encourage or discourage interpersonal learning; creating harmony or discord. Many learners are lacking in personal skills such as initiating and terminating conversations. Are these skills memorising, decoding or creating? It is clear that the loving activities of learning are the focus of the facilitator role.

From the above outline of the roles of learners, it follows that there is also a multifaceted role for teachers. Using the musical metaphor introduced in the introduction, we now consider the roles of the teacher and in particular their future roles as we progress towards an information age.

Roles of teachers

Let us consider the musical analogy to describe four possible roles of teachers: performer, conductor, composer and critic.

If we consider an orchestra, a band or a group of musicians, each is a performer: they work together (often with a conductor) to interpret the work of a composer. They are critical of the composer's work and of their own performance. They may also be critical of the performance of other similar groups; they may wish to identify a new creation to solve the problem that they have identified, or just to give pleasure or raise questions with fellow humans.

Teacher as performer

In much current formal education and training, the teacher as expert is in the performing role. Information is usually provided to learners by word of mouth. When we already have print how is it that we are so bad at using it that we have to reiterate it? Why do we present it to a mixed ability/background audience in an identical way so that few, if any, will find the pace or level anywhere near optimum? The whole process is partly one of indoctrination into the ways of thinking in the particular discipline; the learner needing to learn the code to enable communication to occur with the performer through the written word of assignments or examinations. The onus may be put on the learner's shoulders, particularly in decoding activities, but the learner may well resort to memorising for survival with little real decoding or understanding: the receiver role is being viewed solely as memorising.

Current assessment systems implicitly encourage the majority of learners to use this strategy because they can gain sufficient marks or grades for certification. As we move towards easier and easier access to data and information, the other three roles of teachers have more relevance.

Teacher as composer

The composer role is developing the range of learning experiences. Certainly not all of these can be pre-planned and pre-phased. The needs of the learners are paramount.

The composer will design learning resources from worksheets to a range of books, magazines and other printed resources, from drill and practice computer-based learning to simulations and learning games based on the computer, from experiences with equipment and the environment to experiences with other people. The design will include the assessment procedures, assignments, record keeping and will define the responsibilities of the learners in self, peer and teacher assessment. The teacher will incorporate routines and experiences to enable the individual learners and groups of learners to develop their strategies of learning how to learn. It is not the haphazard design carried out by individual teachers (the members of the band or orchestra) but an overall mutual agreement on the composition, that does not prelude improvisation and impromptu modes. The performers have become the learners with the teacher in their specialist role rather like the leaders of the groups of instruments. (This relationship is considered further in section 5.)

Teacher as conductor

The conductor role is a crucial role for the teacher of the future. It will be about enabling the group to learn how to learn in all areas of learning, how to organize, assess and evaluate their learning. The teacher as conductor will need to be a multi-disciplinary all-rounder with access to specialists when and where necessary. The specialist would act more as an adviser, consultant or leader in a particular context rather than a performer: the guest conductor brought in for a particular problem-solving exercise.

The musical conductor is about ensuring that the pace and balance are right. Different instruments and groups of instruments play at different rates and at different levels according to the characteristics of the instrument. The conductor role is about ensuring that each learner maintains self-assessment to continuously identify their learning roles and strategies suitable to their own characteristics. The teacher will facilitate the group of learners in following the learning design according to the constraints, abilities and environment in which learning is taking place. As we identify in section 5, learners in classrooms and learners at home have different needs which may require as different a design as those for classical western music and classical Indian music. Diagnostic assessment procedures, together with evaluation procedures, will also need to be utilized by the conductor, but these are really the role of the critic.

Teacher as critic

The critic role is one which is shared between teachers, specialists and learners rather than being confined to the teacher or conventional examiners. Self and peer assessment will become more important parts of the assessment procedure. Assessments will be focused around reports presented orally, by electronic media and/or in print. These are the procedures outlined in sections 2 and 3.

Relationship between learners and teachers

It is our view that most, or much, communication between teachers and learners should take place through the medium of assessment and evaluation. The assessment and evaluation can be formal procedures or informal procedures such as conversations (see sections 2 and 3). The assessment and evaluation procedures may have a fixed routine associated with external requirements and with prescribed levels, but it should not be so fixed that variations are not possible. It is necessary to adapt and adopt ideas and strategies which are relevant to that group of learners in that context; no two groups are alike even in the same context, nor is the same group identical when in different locations or with different teachers. The dynamics of the group changes with relative body positions and certainly changes when different members are present; change the teacher and the group is different! Group dynamics also change when the room layout or physical environment changes.

Evaluating and assessing can be used for the purposes of both feedback and feedforward. One of the hopes of the early programmed learning advocates was the idea that a programme could be adaptive. By keeping some record of the learners achievements and errors it was possible to begin to predict which of a variety of routes would be more suitable for learning that was about to be undertaken. This prediction is the feedforward aspect. But the feedforward needs to be associated with a continuous feedback as well to enable continuous adaptations to be made.

The programmed learning approach and much of current computer-based learning are still based around memorising and decoding activities of learning. In order to move towards an adaptive approach, an enormous amount of storage is required within a computer. There may be more potential in adapting more complex artificial intelligence approaches. There is available an excellent adaptive processor which can make instantaneous decisions and has the ability to communicate well with humans – another human! However much computer based learning is adapted, using current or future known technologies there is no way that it can match the human in adaptability and in dealing with human problems.

Why should the teacher be the sole keeper of records? Why shouldn't the learner take more responsibility for record keeping? Why is it that this is most common in junior and elementary schools and least common in universities? If the learner is keeping a personal record, who is being cheated when the next phase of learning occurs and incorrect information is there? Obviously this raises many questions of styles of assessment, personal records, profiles, competency based approaches, criterion-referenced approaches as alternatives to conventional norm referenced assessments for comparative purposes. Are we still in a society which requires a standard industrialized system for an information age?

It should be clear that we see the learner being involved in taking on increasing responsibility for their learning. The creating and loving activities of learning are more important in a world where less hours are likely to be worked each week, for less weeks in the year, for less years in one's life. The role of education as a continuing lifelong process involved in adapting and coping with change is different. The role of the teacher as a performer will become more redundant. The teacher as composer, conductor and critic relating to the learner becoming more involved in creating and loving aspects, but with memorising and decoding as adaptable, looks to be a more likely scenario in the future.

Suggested group activities

1. What roles do we expect our learners to take?

A video recording of a teacher with learners is the basis for this activity. The group of teachers explain and discuss what they see in the video. The four learning activities of memorising, decoding, creating and loving may be used as a basis for discussion. The same sort of session could be carried out with learners; their perspectives will probably be even more illuminating! It is important that this is seen as a creative and loving session not as a critical and destructive one. Nobody is perfect and we all have something to learn from one another. The process is about helping one another to develop and adapt.

2. What roles do we take? Do they vary?

A similar video recording could be used to that outlined in the previous activity. The focus of this activity is what roles do teachers take. The four roles of performer, composer, conductor and critic may be used as a basis. The activity could include learners as participants if possible. Again, it is important that this is seen as a creative and loving session not as a critical and destructive one. The process is about helping one another to develop and adapt.

3. How do continuous assessment procedures relate to the roles of learners and teachers?

Ask one of the group to identify both formal and informal assessment procedures that they use with a group of learners. As individuals, consider each of the assessment procedures from the perspective of the roles of the learners (receiver, detective, generator and facilitator) and the roles of the teacher (performer, conductor, composer and critic). Compare perceptions. An alternative is to use a case study as a basis.

4. What sort of feedback is given to learners, parents and employers?

Using the work of learners that has been marked, reports sent to parents, or reports/references sent to employers, critically review what use these are from the perspective of the recipient. Role play could be used where the 'learner' (having only seen comments on their own work), the 'parents' (having only received the report) or the 'employer' (having only received the report or reference) are in conversation or formal interview.

5. How do we enable groups of learners and individuals to develop autonomy in learning?

Where teachers are practising this approach, both they and some of the learners could give a brief presentation and then be available for questioning.

6. How much jargon do we expect learners to know?

It is essential that the group are from a mixed disciplinary background. Resource material can be handouts or a video recording of an actual lesson. Non-specialists should look for technical jargon and unreasonable assumptions. The issues identified could form the basis for a discussion with the originator, or if material is used based from outside the group for members to side within judgement based on cases made for the prosecution and defence.

Difficulties and criticisms

The stance we have taken has focused on the learner. Most education and training involves teachers too! Not only does the characteristic of the learner have to be taken into account but also the characteristic and personality of the teacher. Unfortunately current organization and administration of education and training often fails to avoid the weaknesses of, or build on the strengths of, the individual teacher's personality. The ideas that we have proposed may enable some teachers to function more efficiently than at present, but teachers who are good in the performing role may feel very frustrated by changing to the conductor and critic roles.

The section has taken a particular stance with regard to giving more responsibility to learners in learning how to learn. For learners already involved in an institutional system where this is not the case, a change will either have to be dramatic (with all the inherent problems of such a change) or gradual. For a learner changing the learning environment the dramatic approach may be most fruitful, but considerable support will be necessary in the initial phases.

As learners are often unaware of their own best style of learning (see page 16) or their optimum work cycle, effort will be necessary over a period of time to help them to find out more about themselves. The focus of that exploration is limited by times and styles of working. Rather than imposing alternatives from the teachers it is better if learners can find out from one another by sharing how they work when studying, reading, problem solving, etc. Again this approach is more time consuming. We contend that the improved performance of learners in the long run more than compensates for the loss of performance in the early stages.

Learners are often trained to work alone, any sharing constitutes cheating. This is a clear barrier that will need to be broken down if the approaches suggested are to be implemented. The losses include less assessment information about the individual; the gains include learning to share problems and explorations with others, not being dishonest about learning, viewing learning as a shared activity. Should the assessment tail wag the learning dog?

The musical analogy for teachers' roles can, like all analogies, be carried too far. If the score is poor in classical music the sound is not pleasant. If there is too much volume from brass and drums at the expense of others, we complain of noise. Noise is a useful concept in learning and in communication: if there is too much noise the message is lost. Noise in a learning context can include:

• unpleasant environment (humidity, temperature, sound)

• assumptions beyond the learner's abilities

• incompatibility of learner and teacher values or styles

• distraction (eg. learner has headache).

Unless the noise is controlled, the communication process breaks down. Also what is acceptable to one learner may be noise to another.

We have suggested assessing and evaluating as a means of ensuring that communication exists. These may not be regular formal procedures, but as indicated in section 2 they can be informal procedures. Returning to the musical analogy, the critic can be reacting instantaneously rather than writing a script for a television programme a week later.

Annotated bibliography

Barrett, J (1984)
Student-Tutor Communication in Radio Tutorials
Programmed Learning and Educational Technology, 21, 4, 333-335.
This paper considers the way that students can hear one another interacting with the tutor using a combination of FM radio and telephone. Tutor and student talk during these tutorials is outlined and analysed based on various courses: Learning skills, Australian Studies and First Years of Life. The students participated most in Australian Studies where they were more familiar with the content.

Bawden, R and Valentine, J (1984)
Learning to be a Capable Systems Agriculturalist
Programmed Learning and Educational Technology, 21, 4, 273-287.
The course described focusses not only on systems agriculturalists but also on those agriculturalists becoming autonomous learners and effective communicators aimed at helping others and building up good interpersonal relationships. The course uses two learning strategies in two contexts. The contexts are staff initiative (gradually decreasing) and student initiative (gradually increasing); the latter involves the use of cooperative groups. The assessment is based around a student and employer initiated competency profile including peer- and self-evaluation of learning.

Brewer, I M (1985)
Learning More and Teaching Less: A Decade of Innovation in Self-instruction and Small Group Learning
Guildford: SRHE and NFER Nelson.
Describes an attempt by the author over a long period to examine and improve ways of promoting learning in higher education. The move from traditional teaching to a mixture of small group work, problem solving discussion and peer group interaction is described in detail. Assessment involves a wide range of techniques aimed at assessing learner's higher order skills in addition to the more normal recall.

Buzan, T (1982)
Use Your Head
London: British Broadcasting Corporation.
The book explains discoveries about the human brain and helps the

reader to understand more clearly how their mind works. It includes tests and exercises to improve reading power, memory, studying effectively, solving problems more readily and ways of thinking. The well known mind maps (otherwise known as coral diagrams, patterned notes, etc.) are a feature of the book.

Cameron, L (1990)
Adjusting the Balance of Power: Initial Self-assessment in Study Skills for Higher Education
In Bell, C D (ed) *World Yearbook of Education: 1990. Assessment and Evaluation.*
London: Kogan Page.
Working from the belief that learner control of learning requires both self-knowledge and knowledge of the learning possibilities available, the procedures described were developed to provide an entry-point to a study skills for higher education programme. Using a diagnostic questionnaire, learners explored study habits and skills through a process of action and introspection.

Entwistle, N (1981)
Styles of Learning and Teaching: An Integrated Outline of Educational Psychology
London: Wiley.
Provides an overview of those aspects of psychology related to an understanding of how learners learn. The book is a good starting place for someone new to this area of psychology or who requires a summary of research findings. Many references are provided.

Gibbs, G (1981)
Teaching Students How to Learn: A Student Centred Approach
Milton Keynes: Open University Press.
The focus is on students learning from one another. By learning from peers with the same problems on the same course, the gap between them is less than that between most students and tutors. Examples are provided for carrying out the process, often using a snowballing approach.

Harris, N D C (1979)
Preparing Educational Materials
London: Croom Helm.

The book emphasises the careful development of educational materials and learning situations to aid and develop student learning. The lecturer is perceived as taking on four roles: composer, performer, conductor and critic (designing learning materials, lecturing, organizing learning situations and evaluating his own design and management). Some theoretical background is provided along with case studies of practice.

Hill, W F (1978)
Learning Thru' Discussion
Palo Alto: Fearon.
A small book which gives a ten stage system for organising discussion particularly related to discussion around papers that are provided. The system involves focusing on problems of comprehension and the main messages of the paper, leaving the criticism until near the end. The final focus is on the group's performance.

Jaques, D (1984)
Learning in Groups
London: Croom Helm.
The book addresses the questions: How can tutors in post-secondary education improve their skills in leading group discussions? How can the tutor play a less dominant role? How can students be encouraged to treat seminars as a cooperative venture? Theory and practice are linked by case studies including alternatives to the traditional tutorial and seminar.

Merrill, M D (1984)
What is Learner Control? In Bass, R K and Dills, C R (eds)
Instructional Development: The State of the Art II
Dubuque, Iowa: Kendall/Hunt
Many examples of learning assume that all students should receive identical instruction; this idea is either untenable or unsupported. The paper addresses the idea of enabling the students to decide on the various mediational tracks and which they will use. Several aspects of student controlled instruction and display selection are received, and a model for display processing is developed.

Rogers, C R (1983)
Freedom to Learn for the 80's
Columbus: Charles E Merrill Publishing Company.
The book derives from an earlier book 'Freedom to Learn'. The goals are to provide a climate of trust in the learning environment. Decision making is seen as participating and enabling students to build their confidence and self esteem and to develop into life long learners. The teacher is seen as a facilitator. The book is aimed at fully functioning people, whether teacher or learner.

Rudduck, J (1978)
Learning Through Small Group Discussion
Guildford: Society for Research into Higher Education.
The book is divided into seven chapters. Each chapter is written in two parts: the issues and the evidence. The book covers the range from students roles and training students in small group work to the leaders roles; also included are monitoring small group work and leaderless groups. The book covers a range of aspects from basic practical matters to more philosophical and psychological issues.

Wilson, B E (1984)
Knowledge and its Acquisition: An Introduction and an Overview. In Bass, R K and Dills, C R (eds) *Instructional Development: The State of the Art II*
Dubuque, Iowa: Kendall Hunt.
The paper considers the acquisition of knowledge, based on the approaches of experimental behavioural and cognitive psychology. In particular it focusses on the ways in which individuals differ in their abilities and approaches to the acquisition of knowledge and the resulting implications for course design.

Section 5. Meeting the needs of learners

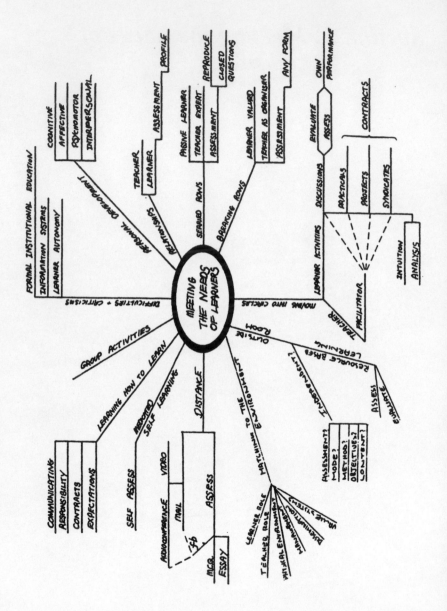

Section 5. Meeting the needs of learners

Section 5. *Meeting the needs of learners*

Introduction

Education and training have particular problems in the design of learning situations. Should the learner be encouraged to only build on strengths, or on weaknesses, or how should these be balanced? Education and training should be aimed at developing the individual to the limits of their personal abilities in the context of the learning. There are four possible aspects of personal development which overlap with one another:

- cognitive
- affective
- psychomotor
- interpersonal.

Cognitive development is associated with the conventional subject matter in education and training. It is the development of the conceptual framework and the ability to apply those concepts in to new situations, the analysis of existing resources and the development and evaluation of new ideas and resources.

Affective development varies from being aware that something is going on, to the development of a personal value system from which actions originate.

Psychomotor development is learning associated with physical skills and coordination: playing a musical instrument, nerve surgery, tree felling.

By interpersonal we mean learning to participate in groups and enabling groups to function; those groups may be learning, making decisions, socializing. The 'loving' activity in learning is closely related to interpersonal development (see page 24).

Personal or self-development is the interaction of the four aspects. It is over simplistic to assume that each of these aspects can be developed independently of the others. This section examines the relative roles and needs of the learners and of the teachers. Let us consider some stereotype learners and teachers that are seldom found in reality; they will help to identify some of the potential problems.

The teacher of forty years ago was probably nearer to a stereotyped army sergeant. A very authoritarian stance was assumed where the learners were expected to remain silent receivers whilst wisdom was poured forth. The learners were probably expected to memorize everything off by heart in order to repeat it word for word without error.

Probably the other extreme of the spectrum is the supposedly trendy modern teacher who tries to become one of the group although from a different generation with different values and experiences. The learners may not be at all clear what is expected from them and have to rely on their own resources and ideas without the guidance that they have come to expect from a teacher.

Considering the learners we can also look at two extremes. There are learners who expect the teacher always to know the answer and to rely entirely on the teacher for guidance, advice, criticism and encouragement. The learner expects every piece of work that has been written to be marked with a clear mark or grade and a set of statements that outline what has been done wrong and how the work can be improved on the next occasion.

Probably at the other extreme is the learner who thinks that the teacher does not know anything, has led a sheltered middle class existence and does not have many ideas about the problems and difficulties that learners experience whilst trying to come to grips with the particular learning. It is clear that there could be some poor matches between the learners and teachers that have been sketched above!

Today, young people in transition from institutionalized education to adult and working life are effectively locked into the educational system beyond the compulsory sector in order to accumulate qualifications and/or work experience as a basis for being considered for payed employment. In addition more and more adults are returning for training and education. The serried rows of passive learners is an inappropriate technique in this context because most of these learners have rejected the conventional institutionalized education or have learned from experiences in life. It becomes important for the learners to have more control of the pace and style of what they do. The planning should be cooperative and reflective using peers and teachers. The use of project methods or of intrinsic motivation can enable better learning. The teacher becomes a guide understanding either the competencies young people need for the outside world or the experience of the returning adult. The teacher becomes a person who will accept their participation in decisions rather than an authoritarian imposer of knowledge.

A working document of the European Community Action Programme on the transition of young people from education to adult and working life suggests three headings subdivided as follows:

1. Individual and personal
- self-knowledge: strengths and weaknesses, mental and physical

- self-confidence and autonomy

- ability to use and accept criticism

- initiative

- logical capacity: decision making, problem solving

- living with emotions

- understanding and development of physical and health capabilities

- development of manual skills.

2. Interpersonal
- understanding of, and feeling for, others

- ability to discipline oneself to accept the rules of a group or organisation

- ability to articulate ideas in words and to communicate, to listen, to explain, to read and to write.

3. Understanding and knowledge
- understanding of number and basic mathematics

- understanding and knowledge of existing kinds of work and of the organization of industry, commerce, and administration; possible developments in the future such as information technologies: and implications for the kinds of personal and interpersonal competencies needed

- understanding and knowledge of the alternative forms and patterns of human activity that might replace 'work' and of leisure activities

- understanding and knowledge of the nature of personal and family relationships

- understanding of and knowledge of society as a whole and the individuals role in it.

The assessment implications in the context of learning can immediately be envisaged by scanning the above lists. Conventional certification with global marks would be meaningless, although some parts of the list would lend themselves to the specification of criteria by which judgements could be made. The criteria could be the basis for a profile, but much of the recording must be in the form of a personal record. The implication is for a personal assessment showing one's own development against the pre-stated criteria.

An alternative approach to assessment, in this context, is to use other learners as the assessors (ie. peer assessment; see page 110). The criteria for assessment can either be imposed or negotiated. We contend that criteria which are negotiated provide a better basis for most learners. The negotiation could, for example, involve potential employers.

Modes of learning

In this section we examine various types of learning situations or models, discuss their characteristics and relate these to styles of assessment and evaluation which will help the needs of learners to be met.

Serried rows

The teacher is facing the learners who are usually in serried rows of seats either in a classroom or in a lecture room or lecture theatre. The teacher is assisted in their teaching by the use of chalkboards, overhead projectors, slides, film, television or other audio visual aids. The whole arrangement implies that the teacher is the expert performer and that the learners are in a receiver mode. The usual method of presentation (a loaded word in itself) is by passing on

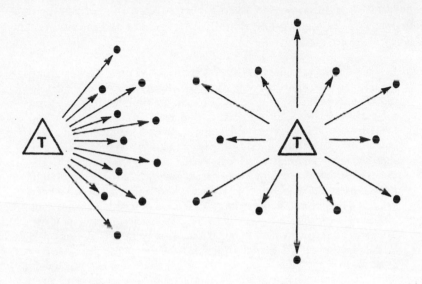

Figure 5.1 *Serried rows*

information. The learner usually writes notes. The partial assumption is that there are facts, a specified body of knowledge or an exposition, which will indicate to the learners the sort of work that they are expected to produce.

The learner's role is almost exclusively passive. The teacher is the purveyor of knowledge, the expert, the king of the subject. The approach tends to be authoritarian, the teacher is the senior partner in the learning, the learner has no real responsibility but to reproduce the expert's ideas. Assessment will most probably ask for the work to be reproduced and for examples to be worked out based on the presentations. An alternative will be where a range of reading is provided and the learner has to decide the purpose of the exposition and deduce what will be asked in the assessment. This alternative does pass more responsibility to the learner in moving from a receiver to a detective role.

The learner is not expected to have much initiative, but to adopt the 'right answer syndrome'. Probably one of the key criticisms that can be levelled at this type of education and training is that the learners are expected to get the right answer, yet as has been indicated in an earlier section, much of life is about finding the answers to problems that do not have a right answer or even a best answer, but an answer that depends on the assumptions that the solver makes and the situation in which they are made.

In some textual material it is the practice to incorporate questions into the text. The questions can be used to check what has been learned (self-assessment questions) or to focus attention for learning. In a course on road safety, the learners were first given 6 questions to think about and to jot down any answers they considered applied. They could also talk to one another about the questions. They then had a synchronized tape slide sequence and illustrated texts (using similar visual images). The same questions were the headings for the sections of the two presentations.. After the sequence, the learners were individually asked the original 6 questions together with further more detailed questions. The first set of questions were aimed at helping the learners focus their ideas. They were questions which could be identified as 'to aid learning'. The learner's minds were partially focussed by the questions. There is evidence to suggest that this is a very efficient method of learning, being more understandable to learners than a set of objectives. The more detailed questions were focussing on what had been learned.

The implications for assessment are clear. In this type of learning environment it is unreasonable to expect the learners to think for themself or to transfer ideas that have been learned in one context to another. The most suitable type of assessment will be the closed question (multiple choice, short answer or structured essay type question) where it is clear that a correct answer is expected. Marks are to be gained by using the expected method of solution, criticism or style of writing. Where the derivation of a solution involves an algorithmic approach, there will probably be only one or two potential algorithms assumed in the mark scheme. This style of assessment is most common in public examinations for certification because the assessments are the most reliable where discrimination is required between the learners. By implication it could be argued that the right way to teach for this style of assessment is to use the style of teaching that we have called 'serried rows'.

The assessment used is often incompatible with the teaching approach. Learners are often required to answer assessment questions with open ended essay questions, questions requiring analysis, even generation of original ideas, whereas the teaching has developed an assumption of uncritical acceptance of ideas. In order to enable learners to cope with the style of assessment, different teaching methods are required, although the cynic might identify that the purpose of the assessment is to discriminate. If discrimination is required, let natural abilities flow rather than teaching for the examination ... what happened to the learning and the needs of the learner?

Breaking rows

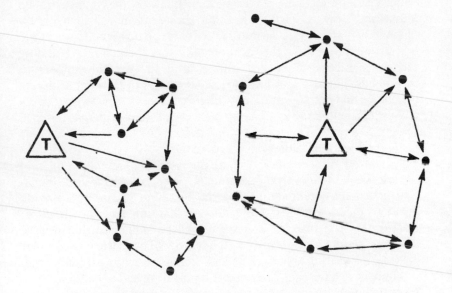

Figure 5.2 *Breaking rows*

Many classrooms and lecture rooms are used by the teachers in a different way. The learners are given an active role in the learning by using, for example, buzz groups with a particular question or short problem. The groups may work on a snowball principle (see page 52), but will usually be expected to report some or all of their decisions to the rest of the group. The first implication of this approach is that the learner's views are valued and that learners have something to offer the group. The teacher becomes less of an expert but takes on a role of the organizer of the activity (conductor). The feedback that the learner offers in their reporting gives the teacher some information about particular problems of individuals and also of the group in general. Not only is the learner using some assessment procedures but also some evaluation procedures. (Evaluation procedures are discussed in more detail in section 2).

The learning is no longer just about memorising, so there are implications for assessment: opinions and evidence to support those opinions have become important. The assessor is trying to elicit the understanding demonstrated by the opinions, evidence and peer criticisms. The multiple choice type of question may appear to be redundant. However by using multiple choice questions with a narrow range of distractors (see section 3), learners can be asked to select the best answers (not the right answer) and justify their choice. Not only can the choice and justification be used for tutorial support to individuals, but also as a basis for small groups of learners justifying the choice and perhaps even reporting a consensus view to their peers and the teacher for criticism. Short answer questions with reasons have similar potential. The focus of the assessment has moved towards facilitating learning rather than certification.

Structured essay questions (where the last part aims at opinions and experiences), open essays, case studies, projects, gaming and simulation have much potential for facilitating learning. The last few provide a better match between the mode of learning and the mode of assessment. The form of assessment will be similar to the form of learning, giving more security to the learner. The learner knows that answers depend on assumptions and arguments using evidence; that evidence may have been provided or it may have had to be found. The learning and assessment can obviously be carried out in groups, but more of this later.

Let us also consider some of the alternative methods of structuring work when breaking rows. Worksheets have become increasingly popular at all levels of education and training. These vary from highly structured, so that it is difficult to get a wrong answer (almost reminiscent of programmed learning texts) to very open (or 'interactive') with a large amount of initiative required from the learner. The learner knows enough about the game of education and training to use these materials to hoodwink the teacher into thinking that he or she understands the material by returning it in slightly modified form in the assessments that are used for the course. In the present climate where more and more assessments are set by teachers, the skilful learner uses these handouts in order to adjust their communication to that which is acceptable.

The technique of the teacher setting the examination has probably been more prevalent in higher education than in any other level of education or training until recent times. A reason for learners attending lectures is in order to find out what it is that the lecturer is likely to set in the examinations. Those who are good at working out the expectations are those who succeed in the examinations ... perhaps a legitimate way of sorting out the sheep from the goats, but not what the learning process should really be about. Many of those who are successful in the higher education examination system find out that their knowledge was actually very superficial when they become teachers or have to apply their knowledge in a work situation and find that they never really understood much at all, but merely succeeded in taking the examiner and themselves for a ride!

Where a teacher has political bias, there can be problems associated with some internally set assessments for certification. Again the learner finds out what the teacher's views are and succeeds in writing to these views in order to succeed. The very clever learner may well deliberately take the opposing view in order to try out their own skills and abilities at arguing, but this is the exception rather than the rule. The example just given is a rather more insidious than explicit form of authoritarian teaching. The learner is really being given no more freedom than in the obviously formal lectures so often found in the sciences and technologies.

It should be clear that the teacher's role is gradually shifting from the controller of all communication and the sole communicator, to the controller of some communication, to an equal member of the group. Once the learning moves outside the room, at a distance or learning on one's own, the teacher's role changes even further.

Moving into circles

The obvious form of teacher and learners interacting is group work where the teacher is present. The group is often given a task with which to work. The teacher may become a member of the group in trying to complete the task. In higher education it is possible for the teacher to become an almost equal member of the group when compared with the learners. The group may well be able to look at its own performance in undertaking the task; the group is then about assessing or evaluating its

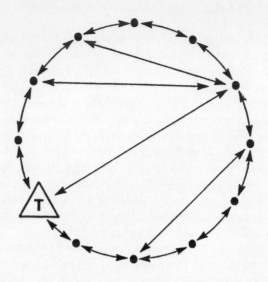

Figure 5.3 *Moving into circles*

own performance. Assessment or evaluation will primarily be aimed at improving the group's performance on a future occasion. It will be noticed that the group has changed what it is about; it is now about the improvement of the group functioning as a group rather than just the completion of a task. In a shift from product towards process the learners have taken on the role of facilitators.

When a group moves into this mode the role of the chair or leader, particularly if that is the teacher, becomes more difficult. There is no way that the teacher can completely abrogate his or her role or position, although some may be able to make that role less important. The group is trying to move towards equality of members with the teacher as a member of the group. Evaluation and assessment that will now take place is more about the performance of value roles in the group. The group is learning about interacting with other learners and coping with their status and value positions and enabling each member to play a part in the functioning of the group. It is sometimes valuable to get two parallel groups to work on a similar topic from quite different strategies. We have found it useful not to warn the groups that there will be any differences.

The whole of a group of learners studying educational technology briefly discussed the role of educational technologists, The group splits into two, each with a leader. One group is given a paper about the role of educational technologists and is asked to use this as the basis of a structured discussion. The second group uses a brainstorming session in order to generate and later discuss the roles. The two groups meet together in order to exchange ideas and are rather surprised by the other group's differing ideas. Not only are the groups encouraged to consider the effect of the way in which each has come to its decision, but also it enables the leaders to spend some time discussing the ways in which groups operate from a theoretical view point.

The groups described above are continually evaluating their performance and the individuals are also evaluating their individual performances. Evaluating has become very much an integral part of the learning process. We advocate the use of this type of evaluating and assessing as an integral and important part of any educational or training process.

Another learning strategy in which the learners are in groups but with less obvious teacher involvement is during practical work where the learners are working in small groups. The learners are given a task and required to complete it in a fixed time. The task and reporting may be shared. The assessment is usually associated with the reporting aspect, although we have seen a particularly motivating assessment where learners are assessed by answering a series of questions at a computer keyboard. Feedback is instant, remedial help can be obtained when needed, and a record is automatically made for both learner and teacher.

In syndicate work the learners are given a task which they are asked to complete in a fixed time. The group may again work on their own for this limited time but then report back. The reporting and the purpose of the exercise will probably be mainly based on a particular problem or critical review to be completed. It is less likely that the group will have any explicit help or guidance in the way that the group can begin to function. Most of us prescribe a mode of operation to save time (eg. snowball) but also to overcome any digressions about the way that the group functions. Unfortunately, the academic subject development often takes priority over learning and using interpersonal skills.

Probably the most extensively used learning strategy which starts with the teacher, followed by responsibility being put upon the learner, is the project method. It is difficult to decide whether this sort of learning is best described as resource-based learning or interaction.

Projects are usually the development of ideas or the design of artefacts when the learner is given much more time than is usual in the educational system. The learner may be required to generate their own ideas or to choose from a range. For assessment purposes it is often thought more convenient to have learners working on their own rather than in a group. We consider this is unfortunate.

Projects can be assessed by one of or a combination of four methods: romantic, objectives, ranking, and collaboratively (see page 114). It seems surprising that many projects are given as individual learning tasks because most of us carry out our work in collaboration with others. There are already assessment procedures used to see how we perform as an individual; why use the project to assess individual work again? The potential for learning is enormous in projects undertaken by groups.

There is seldom any advice or assistance given to learners in developing the group working together, yet surely part of the assessment and feedback given to the group should be exactly in this aspect. The focus often tends to be upon purposes and products rather than the all important processes. The collaborative method of assessment easily enables group goals to include process. As this involves a different type of learning and assessing, it is clear that the teachers and the learners will need to discuss and negotiate the whole process. One of the common traps that teachers fall into is to forget that the learning and assessment procedures are a new experience for each group of learners. If a checklist or contract arising out of collaborative assessing is to be used, it should be explicit and seen by the learner. Assessing during the learning process will be more informal and may be nearer to evaluating whereby the learners and the teacher are about improving the way in which the group develops. The teacher may be considered part of the group for all or some of its activities.

A major aspect of the assessment of an in-service diploma course for teachers and trainers involves 'integrative assignments', where each learner is expected to draw on concepts developed in a number of modules and relate these to their own work experience to produce an assignment for assessment. Learners are drawn from a wide range of backgrounds, and display a wide range of needs and expectations. To help meet these needs, assignment titles, content and their assessment is negotiated between course tutors and learners. The process is a multistage one involving progressive focussing which culminates in a written learning contract between learner and tutor. Although the process varies over the period of the course, and may well be different for different individuals, there are certain common features:

- Completion dates and guideline starting dates for a term's assignments are negotiated with the complete group. These take into account completion of relevant modules and aim to minimize 'bunching' of work load.

- Prior to the starting date of a particular assignment, learners are asked to start considering what it is they wish to do and to prepare personal notes outlining their aims, likely content and format of assignments. Assignments may be written or may be based on multimedia. More guidance and help are given for earlier assignments.

- Close to the agreed starting date, time is set-aside for each member of the group to briefly outline their proposed assignment to peers and tutor. The process is formative and highly supportive to individuals, who generally modify their outlines in the light of these discussions.

- Individual learners and the tutor meet to negotiate a 'contract' specifying:
  - the assignment title
  - aims of the assignment
  - probable content
  - format(s) to be used
  - timescale for completion
  - likely help needed (eg. tutorials, A.V. support)
  - an outline marking scheme relating to the aims of the assignment.

- Meetings take place between learner and tutor at intervals depending on individual needs. During these meetings, aspects of the initial contract may well be renegotiated.

- The assignment is handed in (generally on time: agreement and negotiation of dates places a responsibility on the learner not usually apparent in more didactically set work) and is marked in consultation with the learner.

It must be noted that success of the technique outlined above depends upon the group's dynamic and relationships between learners and tutors. These are developed over a period of time. Anyone attempting negotiated learning or assessment must be aware of and sensitive to this.

Another group of learning strategies involve serious games, simulations and role play. Detailed discussion of these areas is beyond the scope of this book and those interested are recommended to consult one of the books listed at the end of this section. However certain facets of learners coping with these strategies may be of interest. Much of education and training revolves around rational planning and analysis at the expense of intuition. The role of intuition is often not only underplayed but even excluded. In games, simulations and role playing, intuition plays a key role but not to the exclusion of analysis. Effective intuition should be rewarded (a form of assessment) leading to an analysis by the learner of the relationship. Similarly, ineffective intuition should be discarded by rational analysis.

The interrelationship between intuition and analysis is crucial with intuition often providing the potential for extending analysis from familiar limits. The procedure inevitably incorporates assessment within it. Evaluation is more likely to occur using peer observers and/ or by a formal debriefing session where the evaluation is again an integral part of the learning process. Without analysis it may be difficult to separate assessing and evaluating from the learning process. Perhaps assessing and evaluating should be an integral part of all learning.

It is in the area of assessment for learning that the training of teachers and trainers is weakest. The learners on such courses are often told in lectures or in groups what is good practice but that practice is often omitted from the course itself. It is particularly in teacher training courses that we ought to be weaning learners away from dependence on the lecturers and tutors towards self-dependence both in their learning and in their creative powers of generating learning experiences for the learners under their ultimate guidance. The next generation of teachers and trainers will be in an information society. Can they adapt to that world without being given the opportunity to find out, to learn for themselves, and to pass on new ideas to their learners and to become innovative problem-solvers?

Moving outside the room

The teacher may be using resources in any medium from which the learner carries out some study on their own or with other learners, but where the teacher is not necessarily present with the learners. The teacher may be in the same room dealing with some of the learners, or the learners may be in a resource centre, a library or at home. This approach is often called resource-based learning.

The learners in a school are using a resource-based learning approach. Each learner takes a pre-test comprising multiple choice and short answer items prior to entering the system. The test checks:
1 that they are able to cope with the pre-requisites for the course
2 that they are able to cope with the ultimate requirements. Learners who fail aspects of (1) will be required to do remedial work (also resource-based) in order to master the pre-requisites. It is seldom that a learner is successful on (2). When it has occurred, the teacher has provided more advanced work using books and journals. Each learner has a record card. On the card they mark their progress through the units.

Learners do not necessarily have to follow units in sequence nor do they have to do all units. The teacher has a master routing plan which identifies core units, remedial units and extension units. Some units may be carried out by individuals, some in pairs, some in groups of four, some may require a search in the library.

Each learner is allocated an initial unit (most will probably start on unit 1 unless the pre-test has shown that it is unnecessary). The teacher will draw up or give a contract of expectations to the learner and a task card. When the learner has completed the unit they may check their own work against a master example or may request an assessment with the teacher. If the learner is successful then they will be allocated to another unit. The teacher may also write notes on the record card for their own and the learners benefit. In some systems the teacher has a separate set of record cards. At the end of the set of units there may be a post-test in addition to the in-course tests. The technique is often based on a behavioural approach, but does throw much more responsibility on the learner for their own learning.

The learners obviously have much less direction from a 'teacher' than would occur in a conventional teaching situation. Assessing and evaluating are essential in order to give the learners some feedback. Most forms of resource-based learning include diagnostic type assessments that enable the learner to answer relatively straightforward questions so that there is some indication of progress. Many of the ideas originate from behavioural approaches such as programmed learning. This type of resource-based learning is recognisable by the use of simple yes/no type answers or multiple choice questions. The learners will get a response from the book or the microcomputer which tells them whether their performance is satisfactory to enable them to progress.

There are also forms of resource-based learning where the learner goes to the teacher in order to complete an assessment. That assessment may be marked by the teacher or by a proctor (a learner who has already experienced the course, such as in the Keller Plan). Again the learner will be told whether their progress is satisfactory to enable them to move to the next part of the learning. It will be noted that in all the examples quoted above the learners have little responsibility for their own assessment. There is also usually some form of record card or storage where the learner's progress is noted. In a modified strategy, the learner checks their own answer against a model answer and then has to make their own decision whether to continue or not; some guidelines may be provided in order to help the learner to make the decision. Yet another strategy uses what is called an assessment matrix (or geomatrix). The learner may choose several answers from the matrix. After the learner has chosen there is a discussion based on the choice of answers. This provides a less prescriptive 'right/wrong'approach to the learner.

Self-instructional material we would see as something different where the learner may have very limited access to a teacher. There will be some similarity between this and distance study. The learner may make an appointment to use these types of learning materials at a centre. Because the material has to stand on its own, it is important that it is self-sufficient. The self-sufficiency could imply that it is important for the learner to have some sort of check before starting the learning to ensure that the prerequisite assumptions are met. Where possible it may enhance learning if there are two learners working together; there can be an added advantage that the materials need to be less detailed in structure and design because the learners help one another by discussion and joint attempts to resolve any problems.

The management of resource-based learning materials presents the teacher with rather different problems from those in a conventional classroom. It is necessary to keep a careful record of the progress of the learners and where they are in relation to the available resources. Most formalized schemes have some sort of decision tree, record cards or checklist. These management facilities may be operated exclusively by the teacher, by both teachers and learners or sometimes only by the learners. The method of management may depend on the role of the learner perceived in the scheme. It is possible for the learner to be perceived as a submissive receiver of information or as an active detective for their own learning.

The words 'independent learning' are sometimes applied to these schemes. In our opinion few if any schemes are genuinely independent in their entirety. One or more of the following is usually controlled by the teacher or by the designer.

● objectives

● content

● method

● mode

● assessment.

Perhaps it is helpful to remind ourselves of the teacher's roles:

● Composer, where the teacher designs the learning resources

● Conductor, where the teacher acts as manager of the learning

● Performer, where the teacher is the presenter

● Critic, where the teacher is checking the course for effectiveness.

For resource based learning, using this analogy the teacher is primarily the designer or the composer. There will be a tendency to enable the learner to have a clear feedback on their progress. In turn this will tend to push the learning materials towards the prescriptive and also to push the learner into a passive and submissive role. It is necessary to encourage learners out of this mode if the ultimate aim is to enable them to learn how to learn.

The more carefully that the materials are designed for a particular style of use, the more possibility that there will be a mismatch between certain types of learners and the materials. For example, material designed with the holist type of learner in mind (see page 15) may comprise several different sources of information about the same topic: perhaps photographs, video recordings, written information presenting alternative views, self-assessment questions which approach the 'problem' from various perspectives etc. A learner who finds difficulty in moving away from serialist type learning is likely to find this material difficult to comprehend and will probably become frustrated, losing the motivation to learn.

Similar mismatches can arise when teachers attempt to use resources designed for a particular mode of use which is not their preferred style. Many teachers for example find it difficult to use resources produced by certain curriculum development projects which have taken a specific view of learning.

Distance learning

Those situations where the learner and the teacher are not in direct face-to-face contact but only in contact through some medium we have called 'distance learning'. The learner will usually be at a distance but need not necessarily be so. The more obvious means of communication are mail, telephone, television and computer. Combinations of these are also possible. Some writers call this area 'remote interactive learning'.

Mail or correspondence learning has been used for many years. One of the main problems is the time delay in returning any work done by the learner. In order to make the response more meaningful to the learner the response needs to be more structured and detailed than would be the case with the learner who can have a face-to-face discussion after the work or the assignment has been returned. Two general assessment techniques are frequently used: multiple-choice and essay.

The multiple-choice type question has the advantage that it can be returned on the day it is received if there are adequate facilities for marking and communicating. For example it used to be marked by a clerk. but these days an optical reader is often used which scans the responses. Further points for discussion or additional work by the learner according to the responses to the multiple-choice questions can be included. With computer access through telephone, coaxial or optical fibre cable or satellite, access becomes potentially faster and more interactive.

The more common style of assessment uses essay-type questions or short answer type questions. These have to be hand marked by the tutor. Potentially there is much more opportunity to interact than with a computer marked assignment in the multiple-choice format. A hybrid form is called a geomatrix question where the learner has to choose a set of statements from a matrix. According to the group of questions that is chosen, it is possible to generate a discussion type response to the learner. The more sophisticated versions (eg. some used by the UK Open University) even incorporate responses from the learner whether they found the question easy and whether they found the particular part of the course easy or difficult. The tutor now has some further information from the learner about their feelings as well as their progress.

To take the best advantage of the system, the learner in this sort of learning situation needs a lot of help in learning. If possible, learners should be encouraged to contact one another by telephone, by audioconferencing, by meeting, or by having residential periods of study arranged.

A course for social workers combines periods of study in their nearest college, followed by periods of working in the field with a local social worker who had not attended the college course. At intervals there are short residential courses for all the workers. These workers are scattered over a mainly rural area of about 100 miles square with little public transport.

The telephone is used not only to keep line management informed about how the course and its participants are progressing, but also to enable regular contact between the tutors at the different colleges. The learners have a correspondence-based course for the times that they do not have college-based learning. This a hybrid system with the potential for breakdowns in communication reduced at the planning stage and with a continuous assessment and evaluation procedure built into it.

The previous paragraphs introduced the idea of using the telephone for assessment and learning. There have been several examples of this type of work across the world. Much of the use has been in further, higher or adult education.

An interesting type of distance study is where some learners are on campus and others are learning similar (or the same) material but at a distance. In Australia, and other countries where small parts of the population are isolated by large distances from centres of population, such methods are used from primary through to university education. Children at home may receive only correspondence material or they may be linked by radio, television or telephone. Radio and television usually act as one-way systems, although there are some methods of using switching for two-ways, or using unused side bands for piggybacking responses.

An alternative feedback method uses a radio transmission system from the tutor in a studio. Students have a one-way telephone line to the tutor and are not directly connected to other students. Questions and problems could be telephoned in, heard by the tutor and by other students by means of the radio transmission. Obviously such a system is cheaper than multiple two-way radio or audioconferencing but requires specially designed equipment. Evidence suggests that students play a bigger part in telephone tutorials than in face-to-face tutorials.

Audioconferencing enables a group of learners to interact with one another and with the teacher. The way in which this is best organized is still not entirely clear although experience shows that for a group in the early days of this style of contact, a prescribed agenda with some constraints on time concentrates the mind wonderfully! As a group becomes more familiar with the process so it can evolve its own procedures in much the same way that a face-to-face group does. Where there are mathematical, scientific, tables or graphical displays, it has to be decided whether these are circulated prior to the meeting or whether video techniques are used at greater expense. The use of audioconferencing still presents several problems. For example the relationship between the teacher and the learner is a crucial part of the learning process but is difficult to develop where the telephone is the only contact.

Video has two potential areas of use in this context. Using slow scan video, data can be transmitted by cheaper means than using the normal bandwidth required for television. The documents are scanned and transmitted a 'page' at a time. The development of computer-computer communication allows two-way interaction between the teacher and the learners. This enables instantaneous reactions in much the same way that a note pad or a chalkboard would be used in a one-to-one tutorial or in a small group tutorial. The use of such devices has enormous potential for discussion in relation to assignments both on an individual basis or where general problems have arisen, particularly as costs fall and accessibility increases.

Mediated self-learning

An obvious example of mediated self-learning is the use of a textbook by a learner working at home on their own without access to a tutor. The book will have been designed by the author in such a way that is rational to their view of the materials. However it has to be born in mind that the learner is often not the real consumer of a textbook as far as the sales are concerned; the purchaser or the person who recommends the book may be the tutor, teacher, trainer or lecturer. These people will view a book in a different light from the learner because they are probably already experts in the subject area. The learner may have some assistance where questions are used in the text. These questions may be in the text as revision for what has just been read or to focus attention on what is just about to be read.

Probably the ultimate in trying to organise the book explicitly for the learner is a programmed learning text. However with attention given to a step-by-step build-up of ideas the programmed text is most suitable for only the serialist type of learner (see page 15). Another approach is to give the learner an outline of what is to be learned together with how and why it is going to be approached. The learner then starts to use the text with some preconceived ideas of what it is all about. Again the assumption is that the learner is about receiving the wisdom from the writer. These advance organizers are imposed from outside the learner and not generated by the learner. Obviously there are places for both approaches, neither is the right or the wrong approach; a lot depends on the needs of the learner and the assumptions and requirements of the training or educational system in which the learner is placed.

From the last paragraph also comes the idea of following the objectives with questions which check that the learner has been 'successful' in their learning. The idea of feedback is common to most learning designed using a behaviourist approach. In its simplest form there are straightforward questions with a choice of two answers; a slightly more complex form uses multiple choice questions. From the answer selected will be advice on what to do next. A more complex form is the matrix of statements described earlier (see page 161).

An alternate form of feedback is to generate a set of questions oneself before or after reading the text. This form of feedback has the weakness that the learner may be having difficulties with the requirements in any case and will therefore be unable to formulate questions that facilitate the learning process. The next step for this learner is to try and discuss their problems with a colleague, a member of the learner's family or preferably with another learner doing the same learning in the same context.

So far this section has assumed that the textbook is the only form of mediated self-learning. Many people learn from radio and television, from educational programs documentaries drama and even the news! A form that is becoming more common is the home computer with its associated software. Again the software shows similar characteristics to the text except that the learners are usually the sole consumers. The use of simulations where there is not a right answer is also common with the computer as it is in textual form. The feedback is dependent on the decisions that the learner makes. However most simulations do have built into them certain assumptions about the learning process and the type of solution that is better; this may be considered to be more subtle rather than the explicit control of a behavioural approach.

A motor car manufacturing company wished to increase the knowledge of its sales, reception, stores and repair sections in all its distributors. There were two basic purposes a) to prevent ordering of incorrect parts with the associated cost, delay and frustration; and b) to give customers more confidence in the service offered which would ultimately increase sales. It was too expensive to regularly fetch all the staff to the training centre, although the current courses were to be maintained. A form of learning was needed which could be used at the distribution centre but without a tutor.

The company decided to use interactive video together with printed support materials. Each distributor was provided with the necessary equipment. Each new development in the cars (eg. a new progressive braking system) was the basis for a short interactive video programme with demonstrations of the effectiveness, details of the installation, replacement, parts and servicing. The video had questions embedded, some of which required working with the text, others with the materials that had been shown on the video. It was possible to re-access previous parts of the video using a menu-type index. There was no formal assessment but managers were required to keep a record of the use made by their staff and by themselves too. These records were regularly sent to headquarters.

One of the potentials of the computer is to use an approach that enables the identification of problems in the learner's attempts to learn a particular facet of a subject. The idea is that a variety of questions are given to the learner. As the learner makes errors then the computer makes attempts to identify possible causes of the errors and uses other questions to check-out those errors. As can be seen, the idea is interesting because it does not assume one algorithmic form of solution or of learning. However the practical problems of building up such a bank of diagnostic questions are horrendous. It also assumes that learning is about reception. The idea would probably fit into either mediated learning, resource based learning or distance learning, depending on the roles of the learner and the teacher. The idea is one of many potential uses of the work done on artificial intelligence applied to learning.

Matching the system to the environment

The environment into which the approach to assessment and evaluation we propose can be introduced and assimilated is a crucial aspect of the decision about how far to implement such an approach. What are the key aspects of the environment? These include:

- cost
- compatibility
- perceived relative advantage
- commitment
- susceptibility to successive modifications
- physical characteristics
- instructional characteristics.

The attempt will be to generate an approach which, while meeting some of the ideal characteristics that have been outlined in the previous sections, will also function in the real world of the learning environment of the institution or organization. This approach will involve answering questions such as:

- how will the assessment and evaluation procedures be used?
- where will they be used? (eg. where the learner wants and not where the lecturer/trainer stipulates)
- when will they be used?
- how often they are to be used? (there are obviously explicit and implicit resource implications)
- by whom they will be used?
- who will manage their use?

These questions will generate further questions about instructional, administrative and institutional levels of support.

As has been indicated in the earlier sections, we see the learner playing an important role in the processes of assessing. We therefore need to address the particular issues of:

- the learner's role
- the teacher's role
- the physical environment
- management and dissemination
- boundaries.

The learner's role

In section 4 we addressed the role of the learners in the learning process. However the roles that were outlined are dependent on the ethos of the learning environment. In addition, the type of course may also restrict the role that the learner can take. The interaction of the learner is not only with the particular teacher but also with the senior staff, including the senior management, who may well be the 'gatekeepers' for general policy decisions which may or may not facilitate the approaches outlined. There are thus two levels within the learning environment, the sub-system, where the learning occurs, and the supra-system.

Evaluating and assessing may be designed to enhance the learning at the sub-system level, but to ensure resources it may well be necessary to influence the supra-system. Where such influence occurs from on high and at the grass roots simultaneously there will be more likelihood of sustained assimilation into the environment.

Learners who choose an independent study mode seem to have certain personality and learning style attributes. The approach generates a higher level of anxiety and a need to cope with self-regulation. By the development of approaches which require more autonomy of learners (for example, the current approaches to Technical and Vocational Education in schools in the UK, the Enterprise Initiative in Higher Education in the UK) there is also a need for a considerable adjustment to the understanding of learning by learners, teachers and administrators. The funding for such approaches has provided some catalyst for innovation, and intervention, although the political assumptions of entrepreneurship and free enterprise may well alienate many learners and teachers. The environmental assimilation may become difficult because of the horse that is being used to ride the race.

The assumptions of many of the funded approaches are that learners will become more self-confident, more self-reflective, autonomous and self-assured. We have to beware that these supposed advantages are not myths. The evidence to date largely relates to learners who had a choice of approach. Because such learners have these attributes does not guarantee that learners with other attributes will suddenly change! We have been careful to identify that learners have a variety of styles (see page 16). Evaluating and assessing can only grow from these styles; there is a need for the learners to learn how to learn, rather than assume that, because the approach is changed, the learners will suddenly become different.

A further complication arises from the movement towards competency based approaches and attainment targets. Such approaches imply a closed approach with restrictive boundaries for teaching and learning. These approaches also imply a different form of evaluating associated with quality assurance, checking that competencies/attainment targets are being met. There will inevitably be a detailed record keeping procedure associated with the approaches.

However there are alternative ways forward where the assessing and evaluating are a joint venture between teachers and learners. Most of these schemes have common skills and/or generic competencies. Some require learners not only to keep records but also to negotiate learning and/or assessment. There is enormous potential to use the ideas identified in the earlier sections. The ethos of the institution may be a 'hidden gatekeeper' in this context. Innovations and changes are being funded, but funding does not guarantee assimilation!

The teacher's role

As we have indicated, the teacher can take a number of different roles for which we provided a musical analogy. Again it is difficult for teachers to take on roles that are alien to the environment. It is necessary for the teachers, the resources, the administration and the learners to co-operate in a gradual phased transition rather than for individual teachers to assume that they can change the learners and the environment on their own overnight. It is for this reason that we have used group approaches at the end of each section, seeing the mutual support of teachers as an essential developmental approach. By acting as a group of teachers there is also a greater potential for the persuasion of senior management. Approaches to evaluating and assessing have to be designed to take into account the personalities and style of learning and teaching of the main participants. Again we have suggested a negotiated approach between learners and teachers. However unless there is adequate support from the supra-system there are likely to be problems in moving the ideas forward other than at the periphery.

Considering an aspect of the wider supra-system, the actual travel by learners may be forgotten, not to mention the access to particular working areas such as library, computers, laboratories, etc. How navigable are hallways, stairs? How accessible are tutors? These are important issues for the evaluating and assessing approaches.

The crucial environment issues for teachers are:

● the identification of the expectation of their role

● the place of use of assessing and evaluating approaches

● the context of use

● the relationship to the institutional framework

● the relationship to the formal assessing procedures

● the relationship to the appraisal system used on teachers

● how the learners use the approaches

● the role of the learner.

Addressing one of these in particular, the relationship to the formal assessing procedure, there is often an assumption that the use of records of achievement and profiles will bring about a greater autonomy of the learners. The environment in which the approaches are introduced are crucial. If the approaches are bolted-on to the existing approaches (eg termly reports, examination grades or marks) there may well be an attempt to marginalize the new approaches. There is inevitably inertia in the system and stability in the status quo; instability in change. In this case the gatekeepers may well be the already overloaded classroom teacher ... protecting their own sanity and distancing themselves from innovations, particularly if these are introduced from on high.

As we have already suggested, some of the approaches which are becoming the current bandwagon (competency, attainment targets, enterprise initiatives) all have potential for matching well with the ideas that we outlined in the earlier sections.

The physical environment

The physical environment, mentioned in the previous paragraph was also discussed earlier in this section. However a crucial question here relates to the potential for acceptance of the approaches in the classroom, laboratory, workshop, or library ... not forgetting the home! Does the room allow for individuals and groups to function or is it designed for serried rows? As has already been suggested, it is possible to adapt the room to enable certain different approaches (eg using a snowball approach in a lecture theatre) but the actual physical layout and organisation generates certain expectations. The rearrangement of chairs and tables in a horseshoe or circular arrangement gives some physical signals to learners and teachers, although porters and janitors may not be happy with regular re-arrangements; another gatekeeper!

If the approaches are to be used across courses or institutions it becomes crucial to consider the constraints of the individual rooms and their physical layout, or to arrange for these to be altered, probably involving some decisions by senior management, even if only to ensure that the gatekeepers open the gates!

Management and dissemination

The current approaches have plenty of information about what is required but remarkably little on how to go about assessing and evaluating (although a plethora of performance indicators, management statistics and other controlling measures are obviously being imposed). The development of a system of corporate responsibility (senior management teams, departmental/faculty staff **and learners**) has potential. The crucial focus has to be the process and quality of learning, not end-point objectives and assessment. There is obviously a conflict between the co-operative democratic approach that we have suggested and an autocratic, bureaucratic imposed system. It is our contention that the ultimate is not only learning but also learning to learn.

It is in the negotiation and development of the approach that the supra-system and persuasion of change in the supra-system becomes essential. A combination of top down and bottom-up occurring simultaneously is a most likely means of ensuring progress. The grass roots approach without management support is the direction suitable for prophets and pressure groups; the management approach without the grass roots support is the way of sergeant majors and dictators!

The group approaches that we have suggested (which become working groups in an institutional context!) are a means of initiating the process, but the idea of cascading as a form of dissemination has many pitfalls. There may be a need to re-invent the wheel many times to ensure dissemination and assimilation.

Values

As we have already indicated, there are competing value systems currently at work in most Western education and training systems, and maybe the recent events in Eastern Europe will accentuate similar problems there.

One extreme looks for control of the educational and training system, value for money and initiates a sequence of events to enable that control. The use of specified objectives, specified criteria, specified competencies and specified attainment targets has the potential for a closely monitored inflexible system. To that system can be applied rigourous monitoring, management and costing statistics, bidding for places and performance indicators. The crucial foci are efficiency, effectiveness and competition. The role of the teacher is as a craftsman with only minor variations permitted; not as a professional. The role of the learner is as a jug to be filled with knowledge. Education and training follow government decree.

The other extreme looks for idiosyncratic variations in the education and training system to meet the needs of learners and local society. The value is value-added to society by extensions of education and training as a lifelong process where transferability, flexibility and adaptation to change are important. A questioning approach to society and work, not an accepting approach. Education and training are about bringing improvements to society and work and even changing them. To this system the key words are negotiation, collaboration, self evaluation and assessment and action research. Its ultimate could be anarchy!

By identifying extremes it is clear that few subscribe wholly to either. Government and industrial funding for education and training respectively inevitably need control over the system. However as more education and training occurs with adults the prescriptive approach will become inappropriate. With adults the key elements are building confidence, meeting perceived needs, giving responsibility to the learners and developing autonomy. Such approaches are nearer to the second extreme.

It is clear that tension will occur and resolution of tension is a crucial aspect of creativity amongst groups of human beings. But without tension, creativity is less likely. The approaches we have proposed enable the reduction of tension by involvement, enabling a way forward for learning in a prescriptive environment (but with a clear mismatch of values) and fit more closely with the other extreme.

Learning how to learn

It should be clear from the previous pages that we have a particular view about learning and the place of assessing and evaluating in that learning process. Our view is that the learner and the teacher should negotiate the learning tasks and resolve between them the best approach for that learner. The learner and the teacher will have certain expectations which may be very different. It is important that these expectations are resolved into a common agreement. That agreement should involve assessment procedures: what is expected, why, by when, in what form so that there is a contract between the learner and the teacher, any variations in that contract should be negotiated. The assessment or the assignment will be a form of demonstration that the contract has been met. There is no assumption that the assignment is only about presenting a complete piece of work; it can involve the process of getting to any completed form or may only be about part of that process where the learner may complete it if they require but that completion does not form part of the assessment. Whatever the assignment it is important that some form of response is given. The response may be in the form of marks but may be a combination of a profile of achievement and an elaborated comment. In some cases the learner may be required to write a critique of their own work and even to assess it themselves with the teacher possibly giving a reaction to that critique. Another alternative is for the learners to assess one another's assignments. Obviously the use of peer assessment has problems but is likely to be a much more useful way of facilitating learning.

A group of mature learners had followed part of a course where all the goals were prescribed. Their written assignments were judged against these goals. A later part of the course required them to identify their own goals. The learners worked in groups of 3 or 4. Not only did they set their own goals, but also checked and criticized one anothers. By working together in this way they were also able to identify common ground. Part of the assignments from each group were carried out as a joint responsibility. The assignments were self-assessed (some guidelines were offered, although not necessarily used by all) and then peer-assessed. These assessments were used by the tutor. The tutor was involved in the negotiations on goals particularly where groups felt that they were attempting too much. The assessments together with the assignments were read by the tutor. Had there been any disagreement, a re-negotiation with the individual and the group would have been necessary. However the individuals and the group were usually much more critical than the tutor.

One aspect of assessment that is often forgotten is the sharing of insights, problems and strategies between learners. Again there is the potential for a snowball technique where the learners share the ways in which they went about the assignment (see page 52). The development of this approach is towards learning being a cooperative venture between learners rather than something which is private and not to be shared. As a result of the cooperation between learners there comes a realization that each learner is different and that their requirements are different; there are learners' personal needs which may vary from time to time. There are learning strategies to be identified .... whether one is a serialist, a holist or able to vary between the two. Added to this is the need to value other learners' needs and their strategies without an assumption that one is right the other wrong or that one is inherently better than another.

One problem that can occur when the learner is given more responsibility for their learning is that the pace of learning can get slower and slower. Not only may negotiated contracts be required of what is to be done, but also the time scale in which it is to be done. When learners are required to exchange assignments so that they can learn from one another too, peer pressure is very effective for ensuring that deadlines are met, especially if a session is put aside for exchange within small groups. In an institutionalized, classroom based, time oriented educational system these pacing pressures can over-ride the individual's needs.

Another problem is that learners, particularly the more mature ones, set very high standards for themselves when given responsibility for their own learning and for exchange of assignments. There can be a tendency to fall into the trap of working without rest or relaxation both in the above context and to gain qualification for employment. Not only do learners need to find methods and strategies suitable for them, but also they need to know something of their own personal body rhythms and their own most efficient ways of working. Some learners need to work in short stretches with regular breaks, some work best at written work in the morning, some in the middle of the night! Some learners need relaxation at regular intervals, others need 1 or 2 days each week with a complete rest. Some need background music, some need silence and isolation, some need other people around. Learners need encouraging to identify where, when (eg. time of day, time of week, time of month, time of year) and how they work best. Compromises will obviously be necessary.

Another important aspect of learning to learn is to find one's way around the information sources that are available. Taken in its simplest form the learner should be encouraged to look at textbooks or resources other than only those recommended; different learners learn best in different ways using different sources. The next step is to be aware of the range of resources that are available at the right level. Are these accessible or are only a limited number easily accessible? How can one access those that are less easily available? How does one use the sources when one has found them? The use of contents, index, skim reading, checking diagrams are all part of the learning process which can be fitted in with appropriate assignments so that the learner has the opportunity to find these things out. The next phase is note taking both from texts and from the spoken word, whether the latter is highly structured or not. Again these are skills that the learner should develop with assistance from other learners and from the teacher.

A college agricultural course was designed to produce 'autonomous, holistic, problem solving' systems agriculturalists. The assumptions were that human beings seek whole person enrichment through active learning and make meaning of learning as an individual. Learning was perceived as being a process akin to problem solving and situation improving. The teacher tried to design a suitable learning environment where they were facilitators of learning. The learning strategies and assessment were deigned as a cycle of experiential learning. The learners were given a competency matrix in which they had to demonstrate evidence of being an autonomous learner, a systems agriculturalist, and an effective communicator (which incorporated helping others to learn). The learning strategies were student initiated in cooperative groups. The assessments covered a wide range including a portfolio (self- and peer-assessed), quizzes, self-assessment questions, modified essay techniques (also used in medical education) and interviews As a result the students produced a competency profile for use with future employers.

The final aspect of learning to learn is that of communicating, whether it is by the spoken word, the written, by non-verbal communication or by other means such as electronic media or the various arts. Again these are becoming more common in courses especially after the age of 16 ... why not at an earlier age too?

Suggested group activities

1. Can we design strategies for learning (say a maximum of 1 hour of learner's time)?

Individuals, pairs or groups design learning particularly for: breaking rows, moving into circles, moving outside the room, learning at a distance, learning on your own. The learning should include appropriate assessment. The strategies developed are brought back to the main group for constructive peer review and modification. The strategies could then be tried with a surrogate or real group of learners and reactions and assessments used as simple bases of evaluation. Further cycles of modification, peer and learner review can be carried out.

2. How good are learning materials?

Existing learning materials that are used or about to be used should be critically reviewed for:

- learning assumptions (eg. serialist, holist; activist, reflector, etc)
- memorization, problem solving
- learner as vessel to be filled or autonomous
- reading levels
- layout
- appropriateness of assessment
- adaptability
- resources needed
- pre requisites (both in the subject and allied subjects).

It is preferable for two or three individuals to review the same material, compare notes and devise a consensus (if possible!) report which is made in writing or orally to others.

3. How do you read?

You should have a short paper available (say about reading!). The paper should be fairly conventional in format with an introduction, elaboration, and a summary. A modified snowball technique is used. Readers are given, say, 10 minutes to read the paper but are interrupted after 3 minutes and asked to indicate what the paper is about. In pairs they discuss briefly what they have found (max 5 minutes). Reading continues with as much note taking, annotation, underlining etc. as the participants wish. In pairs they then highlight the main issues. In fours they change tack and explain to one another how they read the paper, why they read it that way, why they and how they took notes (eg. underlined, annotated). Finally they are asked to report between groups on how they could get the most information out of the paper in the shortest time.

4. Which teacher role do you enjoy most?

Using the analogy of conductor, composer, performer and critic, individuals are asked to choose two which they enjoy and jot down why. In pairs, differences and explanations are explored. In fours, any attempt at consensus may be difficult, so differences and disagreements could be the foci for discussion.

5. How do audioconferences work?

With a fixed agenda, supporting papers and using telephones at home or work, try it! We suggest a maximum of 30 minutes.

Difficulties and criticisms

Most institutionalized education and training takes place in buildings which are designed to enable certain types of teaching and learning to take place. As we have already identified, the serried rows of seats in a lecture room or lecture theatre provide visual signals of the roles to be played by the learners and the teacher: receiver and performer respectively. How realistic is it to attempt to overcome the inertia and difficulties raised by the environment? In addition, the administrative and organizational structure of most learning institutions is hierarchical and the learners can be viewed as the focus, but that focus may be lost in the flurry of administrative and academic decision making. The view of the learner as the customer or the partner in learning is less prevalent. We have argued that assessing and evaluating can be used as a means of changing the views and roles of learners and can help facilitate innovation in teaching strategies.

A larger barrier probably originates from the background and training of most teachers throughout the teaching situations we have considered. Most of the teachers have been selected because of their expertise as a specialist in one way or another. The specialization may have evolved from their own studies for higher qualifications or from employment and work experience. Because of the specialization, the teacher not only has the role of expert but also speaks and writes using specialist language. The barrier has these two potential hurdles to communication and learning where the learner is given more responsibility for their own learning the specialist has to curb their expertise and reduce their jargon. These are not easy changes, and will need a lot of co-operation between teachers and development of new relationships between teachers and learners. Again the development of assessment and evaluation strategies which depend on these changes could be one means of enabling innovation.

Much of formal education is beginning to feel the effects of falling rolls, and training and trainers are beginning to feel the effects of changing roles where the trainees may have had short or long spells of unemployment. The current institutionalized educational and training systems need to adapt to these changes as well as to a continuing need for re-training during working life. The current 5-15 year lead time from idea to implementation as practised in the public sector of secondary and higher education will need to learn from the much shorter lead times in the training and further education sectors, without falling into the trap of resorting to a didactic style of teaching.

Distance learning techniques are becoming more common than in the days when there were only correspondence colleges providing such courses. The design strategies used for distance learning courses and for resource-based learning may have to be adapted on a more widespread basis. The teacher, designer, assessor and tutor are less and less likely to be the same person. It is perhaps sad to reflect that there have been tendencies to revert to a cognitive subject-based curriculum in the secondary and higher education sectors at a time when the impacts of social and technological change point to the need for cross-disciplinary, rather than uni-disciplinary, approaches. We have already used assessing and evaluating as a basis for suggestions to enable some of the changes necessary. However virtually all teachers at all levels of education and training have been used to competitive forms of assessment. The move towards enabling learners to learn does not require assessments devised for comparison with other learners, but assessing against criteria. From these criteria are devised such assessment procedures as mastery tests, competency-based testing, graded tests and so on. Who decides the criteria and how they are tested? If the decisions are made by the people who are already experts, there are obvious pitfalls. Two of these are: tests which are too simple, enabling all to pass; or standards set too high enabling too few to pass. In between these extremes are norm-referenced tests! In a learning context the resolution is feasible if assessing is viewed as a co-operative venture with learners rather than an exact science performed on learners.

Probably a more difficult problem is the communication of mastery, competency, profile and personal record types of assessments to people outside the education and training system. The use of profiles of assessment for trainees within an organization is already quite common. The use of these alternative systems of assessing as a basis of reporting to employers outside the system is a major hurdle. There is no longer a simple means of making an initial decision. The onus is thrown upon matching the profile to requirements, and the potential of matching someone with a AZBMNQ profile to a BWQHFR job requirement may be difficult!

The final questions are crucial to all that has been written in this book. Is the individual more important than society? Do education and training systems which focus on the development of an individual to fit into society, lead to the scenes we have seen with the Nazis and the Khymer Rouge? Who controls whom and why? Assessment and evaluation are crucial tools in moulding the answers to those questions, but that is another story, the subject of many books and papers. The impact of information systems make instantaneous access to records feasible. What are the needs of the individual learners?

Annotated bibliography

Abt, C C (1970)
Serious Games
New York: Viking Press.
The book explores the ways in which games can be used to instruct,

inform and educate through the experimental and emotional freedom of active play united with abstract thought.

Ausubel, D P, Novak, J D, and Hanesian, H (1978)
Educational Psychology: A Cognitive View
New York: Holt, Rinehart and Winston.
A detailed discussion of the ways in which individuals learn. The book provides much information of direct relevance to improving the quality of learning, from structuring learning materials and aids to analysing learning styles.

Bales, R (1970)
Personality and Interpersonal Behaviour
New York: Holt Rinehart and Winston.
The book is based around a general approach to the understanding of personalities of groups in their natural settings. The main focus is on interaction process analysis but also included are less technical methods which are easily adapted to a variety of settings.

Barnett, R (1992)
Learning to Effect
Milton Keynes: SRHE and Open University Press.
The book discusses current issues of curriculum change in higher education and examines various innovations aimed at making learning more effective. It covers experiential learning, competence, assessment, student centred learning, curriculum theory and institutional contexts.

Bejar, I I (1984)
Educational Diagnostic Assessment
Journal of Educational Measurement, 21, 2, 175-189.
The paper outlines the potential of microcomputers for enabling adaptive testing to improve the accuracy of self-referenced assessment. Two principal foci of diagnostic assessment are noted: deficit measurement and error analysis. Deficit measurement focusses on areas where achievement is less than expected and has potential by using predictive strategies for present and future errors. Error analysis is seen as more clinical and less adapted to self-referencing. Error measurement is a problem for both styles of diagnostic assessment.

Boud, D (ed) (1988)
Developing Student Autonomy in Learning
London: Kogan Page.
Practicing teachers from around the world working in higher education describe their personal experiences of introducing alternatives to the traditional mode of teaching and course design. The issues of student, peer and teacher assessment are discussed. Case studies are given about the ways professional teachers have confronted the issues in areas such as independent study, self-directed learning and contract learning.

Boud, D and Lublin, J (1983)
Self Assessment in Professional Education
New South Wales, Australia: Tertiary Education Research Centre, University of New South Wales.
Outlines examples of self and peer assessment and feedback in electrical engineering, law, architectural design and orthodontics. On the bases of case studies and the attitudes of staff and students, the constraints and validity are considered. Suggestions are made for setting up such a procedure. There is an annotated bibliography of 126 references.

Butler, J A (1992)
Use of Teaching Methods Within the Lecture Format
Medical Teacher, 14, 1, 11-25.
Presents the results of a survey into the perceived effectiveness of different teaching methods used within the lecture format. The implications of the findings upon the resourcing and planning of courses is discussed.

Buzan, T (1982)
Use Your Head
London: British Broadcasting Corporation.
The book explains discoveries about the human brain and helps the reader to understand more clearly how their mind works. It includes tests and exercises to improve reading power, memory, studying effectively, solving problems more readily and ways of thinking. The well known mind maps (otherwise known as coral diagrams, patterned notes, etc.) are a feature of the book.

Gibbs, G (1981)
Teaching Students How to Learn: A Student Centred Approach

Milton Keynes: Open University Press.
The focus is on students learning from one another. By learning from peers with the same problems on the same course, the gap between them is less than that between most students and tutors. Examples are provided for carrying out the process, often using a 1:2:4 snowball approach.

Gibbs, G, Habeshaw, S and Habeshaw, T (1984)
53 Interesting Things To Do In Your Lectures
Bristol: Technical and Educational Services.
Describes a wide variety of techniques for use in lectures aimed at helping learners learn and become actively involved in their learning. In addition to techniques such as snowballing, the use of overhead projector, handouts and tests are discussed.

Hand, J D (1984)
Student Development: the Next Logical Focus. In Bass, R K and Dills, C R (eds)
Instructional Development: The State of the Art II
Dubuque, Iowa: Kendall/Hunt.
A short paper outlining a theoretical basis for student development using learner's self questioning focussed around the learner's methods of learning and their life goals. The focus is towards life oriented research and data gathering aimed at self-education. Examples are given for two universities in the USA.

Honey, P and Mumford, A (1982)
The Manual of Learning Styles
Maidenhead: Peter Honey.
A manual aimed particularly at managers, but of interest to all learners. The authors suggest four learning styles: activists, reflectors, theorists and pragmatists. The characteristics of all are elaborated and a questionnaire is provided to enable a learner to classify their own style. The manual aims to enable learners to develop as all rounders.

Huczynski, A (1983)
Encyclopaedia of Management Development Methods
Aldershot: Gower.
The title is indicative of a specific audience, however it is likely that all educators and trainers will find much of relevance in this book. Some 300 methods of providing learning/teaching situations are outlined,

generally with references to sources of more detailed information. In addition, a framework is provided to help teachers choose and analyse methods.

Jaques, D (1984)
Learning in Groups
London: Croom Helm.
The book addresses the questions: How can tutors in post-secondary education improve their skills in leading group discussions? How can the tutor play a less dominant role? How can students be encouraged to treat seminars as a cooperative venture? Theory and practice are linked by case studies, including alternatives to the traditional tutorial and seminar.

Kitt, J (1984)
Schools of the Air and AUSSAT: Issues in Planning
Programmed Learning and Educational Technology, 21, 1, 318-323.
The paper outlines feasibility studies for upgrading current Schools of the Air facilities compared with enhanced facilities. The latter could incorporate satellite communications allowing a more interactive approach. The paper goes on to describe a particular strategy in one Australian State and how the pilot project is envisaged using ten families linked by satellite.

Knowles, M S (1975)
Self-directed Learning: A Guide for Teachers and Learners
New York: Associated Press.
Designed primarily for adult learners, the book provides a useful resource for all learners and their teachers who wish to place greater emphasis on learning being directed by the learner. The book provides many helpful hints, ideas and checklists to facilitate a change in emphasis from teaching to learning.

Merrill, M D (1984)
What is Learner Control? In Bass, R K and Dills, C R (eds)
Instructional Development: The State of the Art II
Dubuque, Iowa: Kendall/Hunt.
Many examples of learning assume that all students should receive identical instruction. This idea is either untenable or unsupported. The paper addresses the idea of enabling the students to decide on the

various mediational tracks and which they will use. Several aspects of student controlled instruction and display selection are reviewed and a model for display processing is developed.

Rogers, C R (1983)
Freedom to Learn for the 80's
Columbus: Charles E Merrill Publishing Company.
The book derives from an earlier book 'Freedom to Learn'. The goals are to provide a climate of trust in the learning environment. Decision making is seen as participating and enabling students to build their confidence and self-esteem and to develop into life long learners. The teacher is seen as a facilitator. The book is aimed at fully functioning people, whether teacher or learner.

Romiszowski, A J (1986)
Developing Auto-instructional Materials
London: Kogan Page.
Examines the specialist skills involved in the design and development of individualized instructional materials. Automated instructional systems, including print-based, computer-based and multi-media based are examined and their practical applications discussed.

Rudduck, J (1978)
Learning Through Small Group Discussion
Guildford: SRHE.
The book is divided into 7 chapters. Each chapter is written in two parts: the issues and the evidence. The book covers the range from students' roles and training students in small group work, to the leaders roles; also included are monitoring small group work and leaderless groups. The book covers a range of aspects from basic practical matters to more philosophical and psychological issues.

Warren-Piper, D (1990)
Quality Control in British Higher Education
In Bell, C D (ed) *World Yearbook of Education: 1990. Assessment and Evaluation.*
London: Kogan Page.
The notion of parity between qualifications obtained at different institutions is deeply ingrained in British higher education. However no national system to ensure parity exists. How are quality control, standards and parity ensured?

Winders, R (1988)
Information Technology in the Delivery of Distance Education and Training
Cambridge: Peter Francis.
Educational institutions are reaching new groups of learners through the use of distance learning techniques. This book gives examples of successful innovation in the use of information technology for distance learning. A variety of techniques are described, including audio and video conferencing, computer applications and the use of satellite.

General bibliography

Abu-Sayf, F K (1979)
The Scoring of Multiple Choice Tests: A Closer Look
Educational Technology, 19, 6, 5-15.

Acres, D (1984)
Exams Without Anxiety: A Study Guide for Students, Parents and Other Helpers
Stoke on Trent: Deanhouse.

Albanese, M A and Mitchells, S (1993)
Problem-based Learning: a Review of Literature on its Outcomes and Implementation Issues
Academic Medicine, 68, 1, 52-81.

Anderson, S B and Ball, S (1978)
The Profession and Practice of Program Evaluation
San Francisco: Jossey Bass.

Arlin, M (1984)
Time, Equality and Mastery Learning
Review of Education Research 54, 1, 65-86.

Bannister, D and Fransella, F (1971)
Inquiring Man
Middlesex: Penguin.

Barnes, D (1976)
From Communication To Curriculum
London: Penguin Books.

Beal, L F (1987)
On-line Computer Testing: Implementation and Endorsement
Journal of Educational Technology Systems, 16, 3, 239-52.

Beard, R and Hartley, J (1984)
Teaching and Learning in Higher Education
London: Harper and Row.

Beck, J and Cox, C (eds) (1980)
Advances in Management Education
Chichester: Wiley.

Belbin, R N (1981)
Management Teams: Why They Succeed Or Fail
London: Heinemann.

Biggs, J B and Collis, K F (1982)
Evaluating the Quality of Learning
New York: Academic Press.

Biggs, S (1980)
The Me I See: Acting, Participating, Observing and Viewing and their
Implications for Videofeedback
Human Relations, 33, 8, 575-88.

Black, H (1962)
They Shall Not Pass
New York: William Morrow.

Bloomfield, B A, Dobby, J L and Kendall, L (1979)
Ability and Examinations at 16+
London: Macmillan.

Boydell, T and Pedler, M (1981)
Management Self Development: Concepts and Practices
Aldershot: Gower.

Branch, R C and Moore, D M (1990)
Effects of Using Instructive Questions with Flow Diagrams and Text
Presentations
International Journal of Instructional Media, 17, 1, 51-62.

Brewer, I (1979)
Group Teaching Strategies for Promoting Individual Skills in Problem
Solving
Programmed Learning and Educational Technology, 16, 2, 111-28.

Brewer, M and Nevison, M (1989)
Models for Assessing the Learning Potential of Placements
Journal of Further and Higher Education, 13, 1, 34-45.

· Bryce, J, Esdaile, S and Horan, M (1983)
A Criterion Referenced Multiple Choice Test Using Slides as Cues
Programmed Learning and Educational Technology, 20, 4, 263-8.

Buckle, C F and Riding, R J (1988)
Current Problems in Assessment: Some Reflections
Educational Psychology, 8, 4, 299-306.

Burstall, C and Kay, B (1978)
Assessment: The American Experience
London: HMSO.

Case, R and Bereiter, C (1984)
From Behaviourism to Cognitive Behaviourism to Cognitive
Development: Steps in the Evolution of Instructional Design
Instructional Science, 13, 141-58.

Chambers, E (1992)
Workload and the Quality of Student Learning
Studies in Higher Education, 17, 2, 141-53.

Chausarkar, B A (1983)
On Attitudes to a Method of Assessment
Learning Systems Bulletin, 7, 1, 19-23.

Chausarkar, B A and Rautroy, U (1981)
How Relevant Is Continuous Assessment?: A Business Studies
    Experience
Assessment in Higher Education, 1, 6, 49-56.

Choppin, B H and McArthur, D L (1984)
Computerised Diagnostic Testing
Journal of Educational Measurement, 21, 4, 391-7.

Clements, R (1980)
*A Guide to Transactional Analysis: A Handbook For Managers and
Trainers*
London: Insight Training.

Clift, P, Macintosh, H and Nuttall, D (1981)
Measuring Learning Outcomes
Milton Keynes: Open University

Copeland, P (1991)
The Multimedia Mix
Educational and Training Technology International, 28, 2, 154-63.

Cowan, J and George, J (1989)
Formative Evaluation of Study Skills Workshops: An Unsolved
Problem
Educational and Training Technology International, 26, 1, 56-59.

Cresswell, M J (1988)
Combining Grades from Different Assessments: How Reliable is the
Result?
Educational Review, 40, 3, 361-382.

Davidson, G V and Smith, P L (1990)
Instructional Design Considerations for Learning Strategies
Instruction
International Journal of Instructional Media, 17, 3, 227-43.

Davies, E R (1976)
The Role of Self-Paced Study in Undergraduate Science Teaching
British Journal of Educational Technology, 7, 3, 23-40.

Davies, W J K (1980)
Alternatives to Class Teaching in Schools and Colleges
London: Council for Educational Technology.

DeJoy, J K and Mills, H H (1989)
Criteria for Evaluating Interactive Instructional Materials for Adult
Self-directed Learners
Educational Technology, 29, 2, 39-41.

Denham, C H (1975)
Criterion Referenced, Domain Referenced and Norm-referenced
Measurement: A Parallax View
Educational Technology, 42, 9-13.

Depres, D (1980)
A Study Assignment Approach to Training
Journal of European Industrial Training, 4, 3, 14-16.

Dundas-Grant, V (1975)
Attainment at 16+: The French Perspective
Comparative Education, 1, 13-22.

Edwards, R M (1989)
An Experiment in Student Self-assessment
British Journal of Educational Technology, 20, 1, 5-10.

Evans, C (1980)
The Use of Student Led Groups or Syndicates in French Literature
Classes
British Journal of Educational Technology, 11, 3, 185-200.

Farnsworth, B H and Wilkinson, J C (1987)
A Fully Integrated Management System for Tracking Student Mastery
THE Journal, 15, 4, 96-100.

Feletti, G I (1984)
Assessment for Capability
Programmed Learning and Educational Technology, 21, 294-300.

FEU (1982)
*Profiles: A Review of Issues and Practice in the use and Development of
Student Profiles*
London: Further Education Unit.

FEU (1984)
Profiles in Action
London: Further Education Unit.

Forehand, G A and Rice, M W (1988)
Diagnostic Assessment in Instruction
Machine-Mediated Learning, 2, 3, 287-296.

Forsyth, J P and Dockerell, W B (1979)
*Curriculum and Assessment for 14 to 16 Year Olds in Scottish
Secondary Schools*
Edinburgh: SCRE.

Fox, D (1983)
Personal Theories of Teaching
Studies in Higher Education, 8, 2, 151-63.

Fox, R, Luszki, M B and Schmuck, R (1966)
Diagnosing Classroom Learning Environments
Chicago: Science Research Associates.

Francis, J (1982)
A Case For Open Book Examinations
Educational Review, 34, 1, 13-26.

Gegg-Harrison, T S (1992)
Adapting Instruction to the Student's Capabilities
Journal of Artificial Intelligence in Education, 3, 2, 169-81.

Glaser, B and Strauss, A (1970)
Discovery of Grounded Theory
Chicago: Markham.

Goacher, B (1983)
Recording Achievement at 16+
London: Longman, Schools Council.

Guri, S (1987)
Quality Control in Distance Learning
Open Learning, 2, 2, 16-21.

Gray, T G F (1992)
Open Book Examinations
CAP-Ability, 2, 10-14.

Guskey, T R and Pigott, T D (1988)
Research on Group-based Mastery Learning Programs: A
Meta-analysis
Journal of Educational Research, 81, 4, 197-216.

Harlen, W, Darwin, A and Murphy, M (1977)
Match and Mismatch: Raising Questions
Edinburgh: Oliver & Boyd.

Harri-Augstein, S and Thomas, L (1992)
Self-organized Learning in Action
Training and Development, 10, 6, 19-21.

Heron, J (1977)
Dimensions of Facilitator Style
Guildford: University of Surrey.

Heron, J (1981)
Self and Peer-assessment
In Boydell, T and Pedler, M (eds) *Management Self Development:
Concepts and Practices*
Aldershot: Gower.

Heron, J (1989)
The Facilitators' Handbook
London: Kogan Page.

Heywood, J (1989)
Assessment in Higher Education
John Wiley.

Holmberg, B (1981)
Status and Trends of Distance Education
London: Kogan Page.

Hudson, B (1973)
Assessment Techniques: An Introduction
London: Methuen.

Irwin, C C (1988)
The Assessment of Values: Some Methodological Considerations
Scientia Paedogogica Experimentalis, 25, 2, 289-298.

Jonassen, D H (1984)
Developing Learning Strategies Using Pattern Notes: A New
Technology
Programmed Learning and Educational Technology, 21, 3, 163-75.

Jones, J (1988)
Student Grades and Rating of Teaching Quality
Higher Education Research and Development, 7, 2, 131-40.

Kandaswamy, S (1980)
Evaluation of Instructional Materials: A Synthesis of Models and
Methods
Educational Technology, 20, 6, 19-26.

Kedney, R J (1991)
Costing Open and Flexible Learning
Open Learning Focus, 36, 1-4.

Kellington, S H and Mitchel, A C (1980)
Designing an Assessment System on the Principles of Criterion
Referenced Measurement
School Science Review, 61, 217, 765-70.

Kemmis, S (1978)
Nomothetic and Ideographic Approaches to the Evaluation of
Learning
Journal of Curriculum Studies, 10, 1, 45-59.

Lacey, C and Lawton D (eds) (1981)
Issues in Evaluation and Accountability
London: Methuen.

Lewis, R (1984)
*How To Help Learners Assess Their Progress: Writing Objectives,
Self-assessment Questions and Activities*
London: Council for Educational Technology.

Lyman, H B (1978)
Test Scores and What They Mean
Englewood Cliffs: Prentice Hall.

Macintosh, H G (ed) (1974)
Techniques and Problems of Assessment
London: Edward Arnold.

Main, A (1980)
Encouraging Effective Learning
Edinburgh: Scottish Academic Press.

Marland, M (1981)
Information Skills in the Secondary Curriculum
London: Methuen Educational.

Mathias, H and Rutherford, D (1982)
Lecturers as Evaluators: the Birmingham Experience
Studies in Higher Education, 7, 1, 47-56.

McCormic, R (1981)
Analysing Curriculum Materials
Milton Keynes: Open University

McCormic, R (1982)
Approaches to Evaluation: Audited Self-Evaluation
Milton Keynes: Open University.

Van Ments, M (1983)
The Effective Use of Role Play: A Handbook For Teachers and Trainers
London: Kogan Page.

Mevarech, Z R and Shulamit, W (1985)
Are Mastery Learning Strategies Beneficial for Developing Problem Solving Skills?
Higher Education, 14, 4, 425-432.

Miller, A H (1978)
Analysing Teaching in Student Centred Classrooms
British Journal of Teacher Education, 4, 1, 37-45.

Miller, C A (1988)
Questionnaires by Computer
Assessment and Evaluation in Higher Education, 13, 1, 50-60.

Mitroff, I Kilmann, R H (1978)
Methodological Approaches to Social Science
San Francisco: Jossey Bass.

Morris, J (1971)
Management Development and Developmental Management
Personnel Review, 1, 1, 30-43.

Mumford, A (1980)
Making Experience Pay
London: McGraw Hill.

NFER (1976)
Criterion Referenced Measurement and Criterion Referenced Tests: Review of Published Work 1960-1975
Slough: NFER.

Nixon, J (1989)
Curriculum Evaluation: Towards the Vanishing Point
Westminster Studies in Education, 12, 91-8.

O'Grady, M (1989)
Change in Assessment Procedures and Practices
NASD Journal, 21, 4-8.

Pedler, M (1974)
Learning in Management Education
Journal of European Training, 3, 3, 182-94.

Phillips, J J (1990)
Handbook of Training Evaluation and Measurement Methods
London: Kogan Page.

Pine, G J and Boy, A V (1977)
Learner-Centred Teaching: A Humanistic View
Colorado: Love Publishing.

Popham, W J (1988)
Educational Evaluation
Prentice-Hall.

Postman, N and Weingartner, C (1971)
Teaching as a Subversive Activity
London: Penguin.

Romiszowski, A J (1984)
*Producing Instructional Systems: Lesson Planning for Individualized
and Group Learning Activities*
London: Kogan Page.

Ross, M (1986)
Assessment in Arts Education
Pergamon.

Russell, J D and Blake, B L (1988)
Formative and Summative Evaluation Products and Learners
Educational Technology, 28, 9, 22-28.

Saunders, D (1992)
Peer Tutoring in Higher Education
Studies in Higher Education, 17, 2, 211-18.

Shayer, M and Adey, P (1981)
Towards a Science of Science Teaching
London: Heinemann.

Smith, N L (1981)
Evaluating Evaluation Methods
Studies in Educational Evaluation, 7, 2, 173-81.

Smith, P B (1980)
Group Processes and Personal Change
London: Harper and Row.

Suessmuth, P (1978)
Ideas for Training Managers and Supervisors
Mansfield: University Associates of Europe.

Tait, K and Hughes, I E (1984)
Some Experiences in Using a Computer Based Learning System as an
Aid to Self-teaching and Self-assessment
Computers and Education, 8, 3.

Tenbrink, T (1974)
Evaluation: A Practical Guide for Teachers
New York: McGraw Hill.

Thomas, L F and Harri-Augstein, S (1985)
Self-organised Learning: Foundations of a Conversational Science for Psychology
London: Routledge and Kegan Paul.

Thyer, B A (1988)
Teaching Without Testing: A Preliminary Report of an Innovative
Technique for Social Work Evaluation
Innovative Higher Education, 13, 1, 47-53.

Tolhurst, D (1992)
A Checklist for Evaluating Content-based Hypertext Computer
Software
Educational Technology, 32, 3, 17-21.

Tough, A (1979)
The Adult's Learning Projects
Toronto: Ontario Institute for Studies in Education.

Walstad, W B (1984)
Analysing Minimal Competency Test Performance
Journal of Educational Research, 77, 5, 261-6.

Warren, J R (1971)
College Grading Practices: An Overview
Washington: ERIC Clearinghouse.

Webb, G (1981)
An Evaluation of Techniques For Analysing Small Group Work
Programmed Learning and Educational Technology, 18, 2, 64-6.

Webber, R H (1992)
Structured Short Answer Questions: An Alternative Examination Method
Medical Education, 26, 1, 58-62.

Wessells, M G (1982)
Cognitive Psychology
New York: Harper and Row.

Wood, R and Napthali, W A (1975)
Assessment in the Classroom: What do Teachers Look For?
Educational Studies, 1, 151-61.

de Winter-Hebron, C (1983)
Performance Evaluation of Teaching: a Diagnostic Approach
Higher Education in Europe, 8, 2, 5-17.

Zeitlin, N and Goldberg, A C (1970)
Structural Communications: Interactive System for Teaching Understanding
Training Technology, 10, 6, 51-9.

Index